Contents

The theatre is, by its nature, an ephemeral art: yet it is a daunting task to track down the newspaper reviews, or contemporary statements from the writer or his director, which are often all that remain to help us recreate some sense of what a particular production was like. This series is therefore intended to make readily available a selection of the comments that the critics made about the plays of leading modern dramatists at the time of their production — and to trace, too, the course of each writer's own views about his work and his world.

In addition to combining a uniquely convenient source of such elusive *documentation*, the 'Writer-Files' series also assembles the *information* necessary for readers to pursue further their interest in a particular writer or work. Variations in quantity between one writer's output and another's, differences in temperament which make some readier than others to talk about their work, and the variety of critical response, all mean that the presentation and balance of material shifts between one volume and another: but we have tried to arrive at a format for the series which will nevertheless enable users of one volume readily to find their way around any other.

Section 1, 'A Brief Chronology', provides a quick conspective overview of each playwright's life and career. *Section 2* deals with the plays themselves, arranged chronologically in the order of their composition: information on first performances, major revivals, and publication is followed by a brief synopsis (for quick reference set in slightly larger, italic type), then by a representative selection of the critical response, and of the dramatist's own comments on the play and its theme.

Section 3 offers concise guidance to each writer's work in non-dramatic forms, while *Section 4*, 'The Writer on His Work', brings together comments from the playwright himself on more general matters of construction, opinion, and artistic development. Finally, *Section 5* provides a bibliographical guide to other primary and secondary sources of further reading, among which full details will be found of works cited elsewhere under short titles, and of collected editions of the plays — but not of individual titles, particulars of which will be found with the other factual data in Section 2.

The 'Writer-Files' hope by striking this kind of balance between information and a wide range of opinion to offer 'companions' to the study of major playwrights in the modern repertoire — not in that dangerous pre-digested fashion which can too readily quench the desire to read the plays themselves, nor so prescriptively as to allow any single line of approach to predominate, but rather to encourage readers to form their own judgements of the plays in a wide-ranging context.

David Edgar is variously described in this *File* as 'the theatrical equivalent of a photo journalist' (page 80) and — his own preferred alternative — as 'a secretary for our times' (page 90). That the earlier label was not intended to be complimentary serves to emphasize that one's response to this 'mole with the socialist view of history' — a self-description, this time (page 36) — depends very much on one's openness to a certain kind of theatricality, and its use for political ends. If, as Edgar himself suggests on page 88, he has now moved on from a dramaturgy based on agitprop to one rooted in social realism, this is, perhaps, a matter of the 'photo journalist' in him now resisting the temptation to pose the shots, while still selecting those which tell a political truth.

Over a decade ago now, anticipating the best part of a summer's day cloistered in the Aldwych Theatre watching Edgar's version of *Nicholas Nickleby*, my own twin prejudices against long plays and adaptations of novels were quiveringly combined for deployment. Yet that marathon show turned out to be one of the most joyous, affirmatory pieces of theatre I have ever seen — a unique collaboration between novelist, playwright, directors, actors, and designer which drew upon and merged the particular strengths of each. And, like *The Jail Diary of Albie Sachs*, this was not only an adaptation transformed into an act of creation, but also, like *Entertaining Strangers*, a commission written to specific and demanding requirements — a reminder of Edgar's earliest days as a playwright when, as he disarmingly puts it on page 14, if 'people said, why don't you do something about something, I usually did'. That 'something' might, as in the case then under discussion, be a subject as diffuse as the Common Market, or as nitty-grittily specific as the eponymous concerns of *Rent, or Caught in the Act*.

If Edgar was even then probably the only contemporary playwright who could have shaped an entertaining evening out of the provisions of an Act of Parliament, he remains also one of the few, at least among committed writers, who can get under the skin of his 'baddies', to the extent that he understands (and helps us to understand) what makes the neo-fascists of *Destiny* or the poor white Afrikaners of *Albie Sachs* behave as they do. As the title of an interview oft-quoted in these pages suggests, at its best his theatre is thus one of 'dynamic ambiguities', in which the 'right' resolution is arrived at despite a full recognition of all the complexities and contradictions along the way.

Simon Trussler

1948 26 Feb., born, in Birmingham: background 'fairly conventional, more or less upper middle class' ('Towards a Theatre of Dynamic Ambiguities', *Theatre Quarterly*, Spring 1979, p. 3).

1961-65 At Oundle, public school, playing Miss Prism in *The Importance of Being Earnest*, designing *Henry IV, Part I*, and *The Fire Raisers*, and editing poetry magazine *Embryo*.

1966 Taught at a preparatory school before going to university.

1966-69 Studied at Manchester University. Active in student politics, chairing Socialist Society. Gained BA Degree in Drama, 1969.

1969-72 Journalist on *Bradford Telegraph and Argus*: assistant reporter on first exposé of financial affairs of John Poulson. 1970-72, wrote and had performed 18 plays, of various lengths, several commissioned by Chris Parr at Bradford University, and four toured by General Will. Acted at Bradford University, parts including title-role in *Toad of Toad Hall*, Flashman in Richard Crane's *Tom Brown's Schooldays*, and God in Brenton's *Scott of the Antarctic*.

1972 Left journalism for full-time writing. Yorkshire Arts Association Fellow, Leeds Polytechnic, 1972-73, writing for students there and at Bingley College of Education.

1973 First television play, *The Eagle Has Landed*.

1974-75 Resident playwright for Birmingham Repertory Theatre, writing *O Fair Jerusalem*. 'I was a bit snooty about just going round departments and seeing what went on. . . . It was probably useful to be in contact with a theatre for that period of time. It was a bit like being in rehearsal for a year' (Debbie Wolfe, 'Writers' Houses', *Plays and Players*, Feb. 1986, p. 15).

1974-78 Taught a course in playwriting at Birmingham University.

1976 Sept., *Destiny* staged by Royal Shakespeare Company at The Other Place, Stratford.

1977 Began period of activity for anti-Nazi cause, as speaker and regular contributor to *Searchlight*. Politically closest to International Socialists during 1970s.

1977-78 Wrote for 7:84 Company, Pirate Jenny, and Monstrous Regiment, and adapted *Jail Diary of Albie Sachs* (for RSC) and *Mary Barnes*.

1978-79 Spent a year in the United States on Bicentennial Fellowship.

1980 Wrote *Nicholas Nickleby* for Royal Shakespeare Company, working closely with actors and directors at workshops and in rehearsal. Active in forming Theatre Writers' Union.

1983 *Maydays* for Royal Shakespeare Company.

1984 Became literary adviser to Royal Shakespeare Company.

1985 Wrote *Entertaining Strangers*, community play commissioned for Dorchester, Dorset.

1986 Wrote first film-script, *Lady Jane*.

1989 Appointed Chair of Britain's first M.A. course in Playwriting Studies, Birmingham University.

1990 Wrote screenplay of George Eliot's *Mill on the Floss*, to be filmed under direction of Peter Hall.

a: Stage and Television Plays

Two Kinds of Angel

A play in one act.
First production: Bradford University, July 1970.
First London production: Basement Th, Feb. 1971.
Published: in *The London Fringe Theatre*, ed. V. E. Mitchell
    (London: Burnham House, 1975). [This book is very
    difficult to find.]

*Rosa, a plainish student revolutionary, and Norma, a
sexy blonde actress and model, share a flat, but have
little else in common except a shared tendency for hero
worship — reflected in two huge posters on their walls,
one of Rosa Luxemburg, the other of Marilyn Monroe.
Rosa and Norma's humdrum bickering about their
respective concerns — student protests over canteen
prices, the problems of casting-couch auditions — cuts
into and out of episodes from the revolutionary
activities of Rosa Luxemburg (with 'Norma' as her
secretary), and the pathetic final days of Marilyn
Monroe (with 'Rosa' as her press assistant). After a
political dressing-down from the latter-day Rosa,
Norma pencils a moustache on Rosa's poster, and from
this petty gesture the play erupts into a violent climax,
in which Rosa rejects Norma's tender but sexual
advances, and is then brutally attacked and killed by
her. Norma-Marilyn delivers a final, desperate plea for
the love that is all that sustains her sense of her reality.*

It's a highly melodramatic piece, which I can't look at any
more, relying on a series of fairly obvious effects culled from
watching the wrong sorts of plays at an impressionable age.
But at least one had got that assurance, actually to be able to
write a one-hour play for two women which jumped about in
space and time. . . . I think I would find an influence from the
then Bradford school — from Grillo and Brenton, particularly,

in that play. But I think there was certainly the freedom to be able to say, the characters freeze, or, they're back thirty years ago, or, one of the characters suddenly becomes somebody else.

Edgar, 'Towards a Theatre of Dynamic Ambiguities', p. 5

A Truer Shade of Blue

A play in one act.
First production: Bradford University, Aug. 1970.
Unpublished.

A 'short interlude in dubious taste'. Two businessmen arrive at a Soho strip club just before the lunch-time show. They are looking forward to the act in eager anticipation, until they actually enter into conversation with one of the waiting strippers, Luscious Lola of Lewisham, whose moving (and totally improbable) tale of involuntary corruption and forced degradation alters their view — so much so that, when Lola appears on the boards, they beg her, as she reaches the climax of her act, to stop. Having heard her tragic story, they conclude, it just wouldn't be right.

Still Life: Man in Bed

A play in one act.
First production: Pool Th., Edinburgh, May 1971.
First London production: Little Th., July 1972.
Unpublished.

In this variation on the Oblomov theme, the 'hero' Jake, his attempts to cope with the modern world finally defeated by decimalization of the currency, has taken to his bed and so far remained there for 79 days. Ministered to by his former mistress Katie, he proclaims that he is quite happy with his semi-comatose state, and wards off the successive attempts of his father, a reporter from a local newspaper, and a social worker to make a risen man of him. The unprepossessing social worker's 'self-sacrificing' offer of her own body in the cause of duty is rejected, but does arouse in Jake a wish to renew sexual contact with Katie. She turns him down: 'I can't join you in your cesspool now. It's too late.' With several fantasy sequences spliced in, the crosstalk is frequently very funny, but as a comment on 'not coping' the play remains somewhat opaque.

Acid

A play in one act.
First production: Bradford University, July 1971; Edinburgh Festival, Aug. 1971.
Unpublished.

This story of a 'copycat' murder in emulation of the Charles Manson massacre takes place on the Isle of Wight shortly after the 1970 pop festival there. Three hippies burst in on the holiday home of Jack, his wife Margaret, and their pregnant daughter. Subsequent events (counterpointed with choruses based loosely on The Bacchae) point up the futility of individual terrorism.

Acid was a sort of social-realist piece about terrorism — though I did in fact also base some of it very loosely on *The Bacchae*. Kind of jumping in and out, plus a great deal of rhetoric: it wasn't a happy amalgam, although I think there was some quite fine individual stuff in it. But its ending, which has the daughter basically giving the line of the piece to these three Charles Manson-type monsters, I now find embarrassing.

Edgar, 'Towards a Theatre of Dynamic Ambiguities,' p. 6

Bloody Rosa

A play in two acts.
First production: Manchester University, at Edinburgh Festival, Aug. 1971.
Unpublished.

Described as a 'theatrical symposium', this is a play-within-a-play on the life and work of the Polish-born revolutionary Rosa Luxemburg. The action begins with a university lecturer outlining the background to the subject, but quickly moves into the performance of a specially performed play about Rosa Luxemburg's political battles within the German Social Democratic Party, her imprisonment during the First World War, her arguments with Lenin, and her murder by fascist thugs in 1919. During the play, the lecturer and his performers have frequent disagreements about the interpretation of events, and these serve to illuminate the different attitudes it is possible to hold about the play's subject.

[*Bloody Rosa*], though I'm quite fond of it, was an unsatisfactory epic about Rosa Luxemburg. That was my first attempt to set a play within a play, and it was rather mechanical — you know, there was the usual planted noisy man in the audience.

Edgar, 'Towards a Theatre of Dynamic Ambiguities,' p. 10

The National Interest

A play in one act with music.
First production: General Will, touring, Aug. 1971.
Unpublished.

The first of David Edgar's documentaries for the General Will. The play-with-music takes its title (and its opening number) from the mythical concept used to justify sacrifice by the many in the interests of the few. Sketches include a representation of the Industrial Relations Act as a planning-meeting by a group of Chicago gangsters; a school sing-song which culminates in the arrest of the entire audience for breaking Section 96 of the Act; a cross-talk song between then-Chancellor of the Exchequer Anthony Barber, and CBI director Campbell Adamson; and the rising unemployment figures represented by the high-jumping efforts of hideous Dolebeast.

A documentary on the first year of the Conservative government . . . a bit on unemployment, a bit on the Industrial Relations Act, a sort of series of points which happened to fit in with what happened in the year.
Edgar, 'Towards a Theatre of Dynamic Ambiguities', p. 6, 7

A fairly obvious combination of the agitprop tradition with a cartoon style, with one or two quite nice theatrical effects.
Edgar, quoted in Catherine Itzin, *Stages in the Revolution*, p. 141

Conversation in Paradise

A play in one act.
First Production: Edinburgh University, Oct. 1971.
Unpublished.

In a sunny summer garden, a bright young girl confronts an older woman, who sits knitting. It gradually emerges that the latter is the Virgin Mary, the former is Eve, and the garden is Heaven. The Cause of the Fall has at last had her application to enter Heaven processed and approved, and she and the Virgin discuss life, love, and sex, until they are interrupted by a bureaucratic Angel, who, it is subsequently revealed, was the rehabilitated serpent in the garden, and who, due to the Angel Gabriel's sudden indisposition, also announced the impending birth of Jesus to Mary.

Tedderella

Pantomime in one act.
First production: Pool Th., Edinburgh, Dec. 1971.
First London production: Bush Th., 10 Jan. 1973.
Unpublished.

A Christmas pantomime 'celebrating' the political situation after three years of Conservative government under the premiership of Ted Heath. The Fairy Rippon introduces the play in rhyming couplets as the tale of Tedderella, the kitchen maid who wanted to go to the Common Market Ball but was prevented from doing so by ugly sisters resembling Harold Wilson and Roy Jenkins. Luckily, the 1970 election enables Tedders to meet Prince Charmant at the Ball. Enoch Powell is Buttons and Willy Brandt is Brandini.

Tedderella was also an attempt to create a more popular and less factually-based form of political theatre. It turned out to be a very good spoof, and it gave me confidence in writing large-scale parody. . . . I'd done *Still Life* for the Pool, and they said, why don't you do something about the Common Market? And at that stage, when people said, why don't you do something about something, I usually did.

Edgar, 'Towards a Theatre of Dynamic Ambiguities', p. 10

It exposed very clearly and entertainingly the various bourgeois political attitudes for or against the Market; the classical free-enterprise capitalism of Heath (now overtaken by more recent events), Powell's additional overtones of a mystical nationalism to this basic position, and Wilson and Jenkins's different concepts of social democracy.

Jonathan Hammond, 'Fringe', *Plays and Players*, March 1973, p. 50

The Rupert Show

A play in one act.
First production: General Will, touring, Jan. 1972.
Unpublished.

The play takes the form of a church service with interruptions, conducted by Brian, a vicar, who also plays Superman, Lord Longford, Judge Argyll, and others. Within the service, every hymn, psalm, lesson, and fragment of liturgy soon changes course to swing Christ behind the Festival of Light's campaign against pornography and the permissive society. Alan and John, first seen as two squabbling choirboys, join with Brian and Michelle (the lady organist who, as Rupert Bear, also introduces the show) to act out in a variety of styles battles between the forces of 'decency' and 'degeneracy', which catch up 'Miss Whitewash' (the anti-pornography campaigner Mary Whitehouse) en route. The penultimate and longest interruption uses verbatim quotes from the trial of the Oz editors over the 'schoolkids' issue' in a sort of judicial tennis tournament — finally taken game, set, and match by the crown. A neatly structured collage, switching styles and contexts with great technical assurance.

It was an attempt to deal with a subject — sex and pornography — and the Mary Whitehouse, *Oz* trial backlash, in an agitprop way, which I think made it rather less satisfactory than some of my other work at that time. Again, because the form wasn't frightfully suitable, though I think it was quite a good thing to do a journalistic hatchet job on the anti-pornography campaigners. At the end, there was a kind of demonstration with riot police and two hippies being beaten up by them, which was meant to suggest the inadequacy of the counter-culture, and was an implied criticism of the *Oz* Three, whose trial was still viewed by some people as being somehow a great and important revolutionary event.

Edgar, 'Towards a Theatre of Dynamic Ambiguities', p. 8

It was a jolly enough send-up of the Festival of Light. Like a Black Mass with Ribena instead of wine, it took the liturgy of authoritarianism for its structure, and used this framework for a theatrical strip cartoon parodying the self-appointed crusaders against the conspiracy to undermine our moral whatsit. Rupert the Bear, Mrs. Whitehouse, Superman, Biggles, Lord Longford, Cliff Richard, Lady Birdwood, Giles Brandreth, Martin Cole, and the *Oz* trial were dutifully trotted out in a conscientious roundup of 1971's preoccupation with turning the tide of filth. Easy and obvious targets, perhaps. And an easy and obvious conclusion. . . . It was a startlingly effective device to get that audience on its feet singing from a hymn-sheet:

We know there is a plan
Directed from Peking
That we must fight.
Strikes and obscenity
Are a conspiracy
To promote anarchy:
Let there be light.

Robin Thornber, *The Guardian*, Dec. 1971

The End

A documentary play in two acts.
First production: Bradford University, Mar. 1972.
Unpublished.

'The show is divided into three sections, intercut during the evening. The play requires a large open area surrounded by chairs and cushions for the audience. There are also two smaller areas distinct from the main area.' The action in the main, open area is itself a *'play within a play'*, the environmental set representing a school hall adapted as an overnight stopover for the Aldermaston Marchers on the evening of 13 April 1963. A marshall interrupts the foot-nursing, tea-swilling, and banner-repairing marchers to announce a play, a sort of history of the Campaign for Nuclear Disarmament. The ensuing *'main'* action focuses on the struggles within the movement for unilateral nuclear disarmament between the orthodox campaigners, working within the law and the party system, and the advocates of civil disobedience. The subsidiary levels of action are, firstly, the *'Polaris Sequences'*, preferably played back on videotape, which show *'present-day'* incidents in a nuclear submarine control room; and, secondly, *'The Computer Cold War Game'*, which requires an actual computer link-up, and involves members of the audience in responding to specific alternatives in various *'crisis situations'* of 1963. Their answers determine which of the alternative endings of the play is performed — *'the end'* of the title, of a world devastated by nuclear war; or such a continuing, precarious *'peace'* as could comfortably embrace the horrors of a Vietnam. Technically, the play would need adaptation for less well-equipped venues, but amounts to a fascinating experiment in environmental theatre on several levels, with a sure sense of its *'period'* setting.

Chris Parr had this project for doing a series of spectacular events geared to specific environments. . . . *The End* was written for a university with a computer in it, and was very much designed for that environment — so the sequences set in a Polaris submarine were geared to the fact that there was a stage with a fire curtain which went up to reveal the Polaris,

16

and a huge hall which you could take the seats out of, which was the main acting area, and there was room for the computer console as well. . . . The techniques it used of fairly rapid, brisk, multi-doubling, and the cartoon-storytelling style were clearly features that carried over into the General Will. And I think that the most finished technique that came out of Bradford was for anecdotal storytelling — sliding very quickly from different images which would tell a consistent story through any number of different settings or images.

Edgar, 'Towards a Theatre of Dynamic Ambiguities', p.6

Excuses, Excuses

A play in two acts.
First production: Belgrade Th. Studio, Coventry, May 1972.
First London production: Open Space, 16 July 1973 (dir. Chris Parr; with Anthony Milner as Geoff).
Unpublished.

A young Yorkshire worker, slow-spoken, slow-thinking, in heavy boots, with a sheepish manner, stands centre stage, accused of setting fire to a factory which had just laid off some workers. He is tried, found guilty, and sentenced to prison. The trial format ends after 15 minutes and various episodes follow. The social worker, using clichés about anal personalities, is caricatured. There is a family supper scene, with Geoff (already unemployed for some time), being teased by his silly, fluent sister, quarrelling with his parents, and retreating to his room. He is taken up by a girl student, rich and rather patronizing, and taken to a party where he has an awkward conversation with a male student. The actors re-create the night of the crime, with a lead-in with one explaining to the audience that they had not previously done it in quite this way, but maybe it would help the enquiry. So we discover how he spent the evening, what time it was, where the paraffin came from, what the factory looked like, how he got there. The youth is a sympathetic figure — simple, baffled by economics and politics, with the basic human decency to feel that laying-off workers (especially older ones with little hope of finding other jobs) with no consideration for them as human beings, is wrong, and that something should be done about it. Because he is not an intellectual or member of a group, we feel the inhumanity of it the more strongly. The group leader tells us how the actors have done their best to explain and illustrate Geoff's crime for us, and hopes we have found it helpful. We applaud, reach for our coats, and Geoff reappears — angry, bumbling, still inarticulate: none of us have helped, or understood. So he pours out his can of paraffin round the stage. We smell it and see the wet areas on the stage spreading, then he reaches for his matches — and the house lights go up.

Excuses was the first play that I'd had commissioned by a theatre proper, and there were two things I wanted to do. One was to write a play about doing a play. . . . The other element in *Excuses* was the story I happened to have picked up from a paper about this guy who'd burned down a mill, because half the work force had been made redundant — the interesting thing being that he wasn't *in* the half that was made redundant. And I suppose the third element was a sort of constant anger at the way in which people said, I behave like this because I believe in that, and other people said, no you don't, you do it because you weren't breast-fed or because you're in social group E, or because you're educationally sub-normal. . . . I think that was actually a gut play — there was a kind of anger at psychologism, an anger at the view of human behaviour which attributes everything to internalized memory or your ego or your id.

Edgar, 'Towards a Theatre of Dynamic Ambiguities', p. 10

Hatred is . . . Mr. Edgar's long suit, hatred for . . . managers and workers, teachers and left-wing students, futile parents and the misbehaving middle class, and, rather charmingly, interfering dramatists who, like himself, try officiously to probe into the motives of delinquent youth.

Harold Hobson, *Sunday Times*, 25 July 1973

It's surely right that we should be reminded of the raw human resentment the policy-makers tend to forget. It would, I think, be a cold fish who failed altogether to respond to Mr. Edgar's concentrated passion, or to the pop-eyed incredulity-turned-fury of Anthony Milner in the main part.

Benedict Nightingale, 'Ruritania Revisited', *New Statesman*, 20 July 1973

Rent, or Caught in the Act

A play in two acts, with music.
First production: General Will, touring, from May 1972, including
    Unity Th., London, June 1972.
Unpublished.

Written as a contribution to the fight against the Conservative
government's Housing Finance Act, the play takes the form of
melodrama, with music-hall songs, about the Harddoneby
family, who are hard done to by such characters as Squeezem
the landlord, Devious the lawyer, Honest Tom the Labour
Councillor, and the villains — Hiveoff, Paynorm, and Sir Jasper
Pricestroke.

[*Rent*] was written in a week . . . two scenes a day, which included six
songs. . . . *Rent* was the most successful agitprop play I've ever done,
because it actually got to exactly the audiences it wanted and was
intended for. We got a link-up with the Child Poverty Action Group. . . .
It was a very mechanical piece, but it did actually explain a complicated
Act of Parliament in reasonably   simple terms. It played to thirty
tenants' groups.

> Edgar, 'Towards a Theatre of Dynamic Ambiguities', p. 7, 8

Its basic idea is simple but cruelly effective and, for the most part,
brilliantly sustained. Taking the Victorian jargon of the Act itself as its
basic language, the play parodies the Act's aims and likely effects. . . . It
was didactic without ever being dull, entertaining without being facile,
and wittily satirical without being ponderously obvious in the way it
attacked its targets.

> Jonathan Hammond, 'Fringe', *Plays and Players*, Aug. 1972, p. 55

State of Emergency

A documentary play in one act, with songs.
First production: General Will, touring and at Edinburgh Festival,
    Aug. 1972.
Unpublished.

Industrial resistance to the Conservative government, 1971-72, including the Upper Clyde Shipbuilders' work-in, the miners' strike, the subsequent rail dispute, and the jailing of five dockers under the Industrial Relations Act.

With *State of Emergency*, we developed a technique whereby I would bring in a great pile of cuttings, and people would look at different areas and report back. That was quite easy in the sense that it was a chronology play, so we knew we had to do Upper Clyde Shipbuilders. . . . So we'd talk and we'd range around ways of doing something, and get an idea, then I'd go away and write the scene and bring it back the next day. . . . *State of Emergency* ran for eighteen months, being done two or three times a week. So a hell of a lot of people saw it. Those plays weren't as flash-in-the-pan as they might have been. But, yes, they're dead now.

> Edgar, 'Towards a Theatre of Dynamic Ambiguities', p. 7

It was Living Newspaper basically, with much less cartoon imagery, a stronger developing side. A lot of it was yesterday's headlines and therefore, because we didn't have any historical perspective, historically significant things like the miners' strike got swamped by quite small incidents. But there were some good scenes. There were two ridiculously over-articulate working-to-rule railwaymen, standing on the platform explaining the difficulties of moving off. There was a graphic sequence about the dock strike explaining the complicated issue of containerization, using cardboard boxes. There was a scene about a guy who refused to join the AUEW on religious grounds, who came with his cross and got attacked. And we did Sir John Donaldson, Chairman of the Industrial Relations Court, as a schoolmaster.

> Edgar, quoted in Catherine Itzin, *Stages in the Revolution*, p. 142

I did see (and like) David Edgar's *State of Emergency*, clowning-and-song in celebration of working-class militancy and scorn of Tory repression —
> *Basha basha basha union, my heart says to me*
> *Drinka drinka drinka pint of school milk, and see it's not free.*
> Benedict Nightingale, 'The Fringe and Beyond',
> *New Statesman*, 1 Sept. 1972, p. 296

England's Ireland

A documentary play in two acts, written in collaboration with Tony Bicât, Howard Brenton, Brian Clark, Francis Fuchs, David Hare, and Snoo Wilson.
First production: by Shoot, Mickery Th., Amsterdam, Sept. 1972.
First London production: Royal Court Th., 2 Oct. 1972, and Round House, 9 Oct., both for one night; toured to Glasgow, Lancaster, and Nottingham.
Unpublished.

Twenty scenes with songs, designed to force more awareness of the origins and nature of the Irish troubles upon British audiences.

It was an absolutely wonderful experience — you know, here was I, coming out of journalism to be a full-time writer, and the first thing I do is work with at least three or four of the writers whom I most admired.
Edgar, 'Towards a Theatre of Dynamic Ambiguities', p. 7

Road to Hanoi

A ten-minute play.
First production: as part of *Point 101*, by Paradise Foundry, Oct. 1972.
Unpublished.

Based on Bob Hope's 1971 visit to Laos, to try to secure a visa to visit Hanoi, and his attempt to buy American prisoners of war back from the North Vietnamese. Takes the form of a Hope-Crosby Road *movie.*

Death Story

A play in two acts.

21

First production: Birmingham Repertory Th. Studio, Nov. 1972
   (dir. Christopher Honer).
First London production: New End, Nov. 1975 (dir. Robert Walker;
   with Carina Wyeth as Juliet).
First New York production: Manhattan Th. Club, 23 Mar. 1975 (dir.
   Carole Rothman).
Unpublished.

---

*A reworking of the Romeo and Juliet story, set in an historically
imprecise Verona. Here, the underprivileged Montagues are
'anyone who was here before the others arrived', while the
Capulets are the leading family among the immigrants who have
taken control of the city's business life and bureaucracy. There
are constant eruptions of violence between the 'Montags' and
the 'Capel', as they are dubbed by the military in its attempt to
preserve an uneasy peace by keeping the Montags in 'a state
of passivity' (because they 'have the least interest in the
maintenance of the status quo and . . . the greatest interest in
disorder'). Mercutio, whose running contest in obscene jokes
with Benvolio threads through the first half of the play, helps to
engineer a confrontation between Tybalt and Romeo, ostensibly
over Romeo's gate-crashing of the Capel party where he has
fallen in love with Juliet — but in reality to enable Mercutio
himself to kill Tybalt, whom the military regard as a
troublemaker. In the event, Tybalt kills Mercutio, and it is
Romeo who shoots Tybalt dead — precipitating widespread
Capulet violence against the Montague areas, which enables the
politicians to declare martial law. Romeo, a failure in bed with
Juliet, throws himself into the Montague cause, but is persuaded
to visit the supposedly dying Juliet in hospital, the Priest hoping
to effect a symbolic reconciliation between the communities. But
the Colonel tries to arrest Romeo, and as he fights for his
freedom a bullet fired by an attendant soldier kills the Colonel
instead. A curious, sometimes opaque allegory about 'sectarian
violence' and the way in which it is exploited by the
'peacekeeping' forces, military and political.*

The first half of *Death Story* is me saying, I think the original is about
this, and the second half of the play is me saying, I don't think the

original is relevant. Because *Romeo and Juliet* only works if there is a strong sense, not of, are they going to get away with it, but of, how on earth is the play going to kill them? And I think that's a brilliant dramatic device of Shakespeare's — that you actually are desperate, in all those melodramatic twists and turns, for it to come wrong at the end, because of what's been set up in the first half, which is about this extraordinary little girl who dreams about fucking in a charnel house, the whole connection between sex and death. . . . In our own age, I think there is only one force that can get a sufficient head of steam for the second half of the play to work, and that is sex. . . . I felt very strongly that it was a play about sex, and my own play was a kind of coming together of that with a story on the *Tonight* programme about a Catholic-Protestant romance in Northern Ireland.

Edgar, 'Towards a Theatre of Dynamic Ambiguities', p. 11-12

In blandly retelling the story of Romeo and Juliet we sense political wanness — a very moderate moderate's night out in a Verona where the Capulets are loosely identified with capitalism and the Montagues are lower-class outsiders. But even such political directions are lost in Jane Ripley's expressionistically negative set with its collection of doors leading nowhere and newspapers glued on white surfaces. This is a no-man's-land where Mercutio is a compulsive seeker of dirty jokes. . . . Edgar moves the play in familiar directions and towards its predictable destination without much pointing up of anything.

Nicholas de Jongh, *The Guardian*, Nov. 1975

Unfortunately, Edgar makes the big mistake of employing a sub-Ruritanian no-man's-land peopled by Montags and Capules, in which parallels drawn from Ireland (conflict as religious and social bigotry) rub shoulders quite shamelessly with bland statements about class structures.

Steve Grant, *Plays and Players*, Feb. 1976, p. 35

The author uncompromisingly turns to Marx, and even Freud, in his updated version of a simple love, doomed by political manipulation and stubborn human division. David Edgar is above all a political writer. He measures the Capulets and Montagues wholly by their possessions. He believes in the revolutionary class struggle. Audaciously — and not too successfully — he sends up the final death scene to drive the point brutally home. On at least three levels, this is a theatrically compelling play; it is also unforgiveably bad. The theatricality shows how well Mr.

Edgar can already use a stage. . . . It is a pity that the intellectual quality is uneven and he is apt to plunge into naivety at times. His soap-opera bedroom scene, with Juliet clutching the virgin sheets tight around her nude body, and Romeo, glumly remorseful at his failure to make it, is a calculated dramatic risk which fractionally fails. So, theoretically, might the extraordinarily powerful 'sexual' inquisition of Juliet that closes the first act. It could not be more explicit, and we find ourselves eavesdropping and watching in embarrassment at her humiliation. But it works.

David Foot, *The Guardian*, Mar. 1973,
on the Bristol production

Not with a Bang but a Whimper

A documentary play in two acts, with songs.
First production: Leeds Polytechnic, Nov. 1972.
Unpublished.

Treatment of various ecology-related issues, including the flight of Adam and Eve in Spaceship Earth, the true story of Kenneth Hahn's battle with Ford over exhaust pollution, a gardening tale of the dangers of pesticides, and a World Natural Resources Game, played on a huge map.

A Fart for Europe

A play in one act, written in collaboration with Howard Brenton.
First production: Th. Upstairs, Royal Court, London, 18. Jan. 1973 (dir. Chris Parr).
Unpublished.

It started with a send-up of a scene from King Lear *. . . with sallies at the relevance of string quartets and Goethe to the needs of the working class and displaying a left-wing, anti-EEC Labour MP in the role of Poor Tom, with traumas at finding himself using the same chauvinistic objections to the Common Market as Enoch Powell. It then moved on to two smooth, right-*

wing businessmen (played by Hugh Hastings and Jeremy Child, both first-rate) analyzing why European capital will prosper by removing all tariff restrictions amongst itself and setting up trade walls against the rest of the world; and how much easier it will be for British-based firms to circumvent difficult, militant trade unions by moving their operations to places where organized labour is weak, like Sicily. It finished by showing the businessmen trying to keep the worker (Alun Armstrong) at bay, first by bread and circuses (Like 'Fanfare to Europe') and then by naked repression.

> Jonathan Hammond, 'Fringe',
> *Plays and Players*, Mar. 1973, p. 50

Consists of little more than execrations, statistics, strike threats, and anti-cultural rhetorical questions (my favourite: 'What has Goethe's *Faust* ever done for the working class?'), and has as much theatrical validity as a wall poster in a factory lavatory.

> Robert Brustein, *The Observer*, 21 Jan. 1973, p. 32

Gangsters

A play in one act.
First production: Soho Poly, London, 13 Feb. 1973 (dir. John Tordoff);
    adapted as *Sanctuary*, Scotttish TV, Dec. 1973.
Unpublished.

A couple of small-time crooks sit in a transport caff after bringing off their latest coup — robbing a sub-post office of £79. But times aren't what they were — and there's virtually nothing in the papers. The leader of the pair lives in a dream of big-time crime, Chicago-style. John Blythe gives him a delicious shabby gentility with a 1930s-style Italianate top-dressing, while Ken Parry as his blubbery sidekick quivers with dismay and apprehension as the master-criminal manqué allows himself to be conned out of their hard-won prize-money and fails to get arrested by a visiting policeman who does nothing but complain about the policeman's lot.

> Randall Craig, 'Experimental', *Drama*, Spring 1973, p. 43

Up Spaghetti Junction

One scene contributed to a documentary play about Birmingham.
First production: Birmingham Repertory Th., Feb. 1973.
Unpublished.

Scene about the Chamberlain family, ending in Neville's 'piece of paper' speech on his return from the Munich talks with Hitler in 1938.

Baby Love

A play in five scenes.
First production: Leeds Playhouse, 16 Mar. 1973 (dir. Jim Duckett).
First London production: Soho Poly, 28 May 1973 (dir. James O'Brien; with Patti Love as Eileen).
Television production: 'Play for Today', BBC, 7 Nov. 1974 (dir. Barry Davis; with Patti Love as Eileen).
Published: in *Shorts* (Nick Hern Books, 1989).

Eileen — twenty, single, estranged from her parents, pregnant by a Pakistani — loses her baby and steals one. Soon she is caught, imprisoned, and investigated by social workers.

That was a gut play, because I was very deeply angered by the Pauline Jones 'baby-snatching' case [in October 1971 Jones, scarred by her upbringing, was imprisoned for three years for taking a baby: widespread protest eventually had the sentence reduced] — though I should say that the play was based on a number of cases, not just that one. I think also that at the time I was actually living the play's own ambience — that strange combination of Asians, déclassé, sub-proletarian people, and students, in that environment which is very much the centre of Bradford, with very little conventional, young working-class life within it. The character of Eileen really came out of that. And I was also interested in doing something which made a positive statement, which was that although she eventually got drugged out, she did actually defeat that ambience. . . . Eileen is the same character as Geoff in *Excuses*, though what she had, which Geoff didn't, was a kind of wit and social competence and sparkiness. . . . I have written some good women, I think — Eileen in *Baby Love*, and Mary Barnes.

Edgar, 'Towards a Theatre of Dynamic Ambiguities', p. 12, 13, 17

Edgar's powerful play argues that no one has yet learned how to look at the girl at the centre of such tragedies as an individual. And within sixty minutes of emotion as Eileen Millet loses a baby and also her last straw of a desperate hold on identity, she is shown in both her social and her individual personae. Patti Love gives a strong performance as an obstinate, independent, and coarsely funny Northern girl. . . . We can feel no sentimental pity for her. The play focuses her conflict on the battle between a wayward individual and the impervious, unmoving establishment figures. . . . As a documentary drama there is a compulsion, in the last and important scene, to fill in all the background material. This curiously belaboured and stylized trick (characters in the wings add comments to the proceedings) is inconsistent with the rest of the production, and serves to offload too much blame on 'society'.

Carol Dix, *The Guardian*, 13 June 1973

The Eagle Has Landed

A 30-minute play for television, adapted and expanded for the stage.
Television production: Granada, 4 Apr. 1973.
First stage production: Liverpool University, Nov. 1973.
Unpublished.

In both the television and stage versions, the play opens with a family watching a moon-landing on television, during which it gradually becomes clear that the Mission Commander is none other than Lt. William Calley, of the My Lai massacre in Vietnam. In the stage version, the watching family is American, and visited by an escaped Charles Manson (in the tow of the daughter of the house). In the television version, the watching family is English, and the daughter is heavily into the more mystic implications of the moon landing. In both versions, the play ends with the astronauts landing on the lawn, entering the watching house, and murdering the occupants.

The Case of the Workers' Plane

Documentary in two acts, with music.
First production: Bristol New Vic, June 1973; in a shorter version, as
  Concorde Cabaret, Avon Touring Company, Jan. 1975; transmitted
  by Harlech TV, Oct. 1975.
Unpublished.

*Paul Moriarty, well cast as a tough private eye who is hired to
discover the facts about this Anglo-French enterprise, has a
series of wittily-contrived adventures with mad boffins, Russian
spies, and a godfather-style Nixon ('If no-one would buy a used
car from me', he raps, in the West Region's entry for the sick
joke of the year contest, 'Just ask JFK how many girls would
take a lift from his brother'), punctuated by trips to his favourite
cabaret show, the Filton Follies, whose chorus girls have a neat
line in informative ditties. Facts we certainly get, beginning with
the origins of the BAC as an offshoot of the Bristol Tramway
Corporation in 1910 (an early mark of doom, I think) and
leading up to the present tale of escalating costs and interlocking company directorships — all backed up with a massive
take-home dossier handed out at the door. But as a good
Socialist [Edgar] comes down in the end on the side of the
workers, underplaying the environmental objections to the plane
and pleading for the nationalization of Concorde.*
        Michael Anderson, 'Bristol', *Plays and Players*, Aug. 1973, p. 66

I researched it in about a month, actually on the ground, getting a
fairly comprehensive knowledge of all that was necessary to write that
play.... *Workers' Plane* was a very unhappy show and I felt after it that
you just couldn't do committed shows with rep. actors.
        Edgar, 'Towards a Theatre of Dynamic Ambiguities', p. 4, 13

Liberated Zone

A play in one act.
First production: Bingley College of Education, June 1973; National
  Student Drama Festival, Cardiff, Dec. 1973. *Unpublished.*

Strip-cartoon sketches about women's oppression in history and literature, including a beauty competition between the six wives of Henry VIII, a parody marriage service, and a sex education lesson by Freud.

Achieved the impossible feat of making Women's Liberation a boring and trivial topic, except for its last five minutes, when theatre took over from ideology.

Noel Witts, *Times Higher Education Supplement*, 25 Jan. 1974, p. 14

Operation Iskra

A play in three acts.
First production: Paradise Foundry, touring, including King's Head, London, Sept. 1973, and Bush Th., London, Feb. 1974 (dir. Chris Parr).
Unpublished.

Set in the (then) future summer of 1977, the existing text of the play is a partial conflation of the original and performed versions, which Edgar states would be further revised in the light of the actual political situation in the event of a new production. Iskra, the revolutionary newspaper edited by Lenin, now stands for the Insurrectionary Commandoes of the Red Army, a well-disciplined urban guerilla group which is the only major survivor in Britain of various anti-terrorist clampdowns of the mid-1970s. A strike by 'unregistered' (under the actual but repealed Industrial Relations Act of 1971) power workers coincides with the trial of Paula for planting a bomb in a boutique: one Iskra cell, comprising Silo, Alex, and Jan (the first two of whom we see realistically simulating police inter-rogation), plans to sabotage the power station's computer controls as soon as the inevitable guilty verdict is announced. Sarah, apparently a trainee at a counter-insurgency college in Bodmin, has in fact been long-maturing a plot to kidnap Chandler, its chief: he is held hostage for Paula's release, and shot when the deadline expires. The complex plotting supports a forbidding vision of Britain as an emergent corporate state; and the three-way dialectic — between various representatives of established order; among the revolutionaries themselves; and between the guerillas and their opponents, both in court and in the kidnap scenes — helps to interweave intellectual strands which are far from simplistic.

With *Iskra* I suppose the obvious key decision was to give myself the freedom of using 'faction'. I think that was a much more important decision than setting it in the future — to take real events, but to set them in time slightly off-centre. So what one might call the texture is authentic, in that I'm trying to make them talk and behave like I believed people in the Angry Brigade and the counter-insurgency people did talk and behave, but to do that in a fictional way. The other thing, which I suppose is connected with the parody instinct, was to use an existing form, in this case the thriller, in order to make a point by undermining its precepts. . . . I think to choose the thriller form for *Iskra* was quite a good decision, which worked.

Edgar, 'Towards a Theatre of Dynamic Ambiguities', p. 14

Like Howard Brenton in *Magnificence*, Mr. Edgar sets out to discover the causes of revolutionary violence: like him he also shows the bomb-throwers partially defeated by their own tactical incompetence. But his main conclusion is that militant terrorism will inevitably follow on the gradual suppression of personal liberties; and he dates the start of this to the late 'sixties. . . . His play does raise important questions about the dangers to our society deriving from the erosion of personal liberties. Personally I think he is much too soft on his urban guerilla cell who seem to be all acting out of the highest political motives. . . . Also his chief Establishment spokesman, a Brigadier in charge of counter-intelligence operations in Bodmin, is straight out of the Aftermyth of War sketch in *Beyond the Fringe*. But although the play views the subject of terrorism with a slightly one-eyed stance, it does at least make the point that violence never springs out of a void but derives from a complex chain of cause and effect.

Michael Billington, *The Guardian*, 6 Sept. 1973

Works effectively as political melodrama, but its psychological structure is shaky. Since the play is fuelled by the dissensions among its revolutionary characters, it is unfortunate that they can hardly be told apart.

Robert Cushman, *The Observer*, 3 Feb. 1974

Dick Deterred

A burlesque play in two acts, with songs.
First production: Bush Th., London, 25 Feb. 1974; trans. to ICA Th., London, 5 Mar. 1974 (dir. Michael Wearing).
First New York production: No Smoking Playhouse (Redfield Th.), 13 Jan. 1983 (dir. George Wolf Reily).
Published: New York; London: Monthly Review Press, 1974.

[Based on Shakespeare's Richard III] *Edgar's first achievement has been to discover in Shakespeare's play enough parallels to cover an extraordinary amount of recent American history. Clarence's nightmare in the Tower becomes McCarthy walled up in the Hilton during the Chicago convention; the murder of the little princes is the actual bugging of Watergate; Nixon's visits to Brezhnev and Mao are likened to the scene where Richard parades with two bishops before the citizens of London; while the accusing ghosts who appear to Richard before the Battle of Bosworth are those of Mitchell, Haldeman, John Dean, and all. The ingenuity of the comparisons keeps the audience constantly on the alert. Finally, Dick de Turd is isolated on the battlefield, crying out: 'My kingdom for a (scape)goat.' . . . With Shakespeare to help him, Edgar's free-flowing imagination acquires shape without losing its freedom. . . .*

The band was perched precariously above an adaptable inner stage, like a convention band, while the auditorium was painted with the Stars and Stripes as its motif. Sue Plummer, the designer, surrounded us with the atmosphere of a political convention in the States, so that the Elizabethan costumes, and particularly Gregory Floy's limping deformed Dick, with his Olivier mannerisms, stood out in greater contrast. This contrast also emerged in the dialogue, half-Shakespearian blank verse, half-huckster slang.

John Elsom, 'Edgar's Goat',
The Listener, 7 Mar. 1974, p. 316

The Dunkirk Spirit

A full-length play, with music.
First production: touring, by General Will, Jan. 1974.
Unpublished.

This, the third and last in a series of plays about the Conservative government of 1970-74 for General Will, traces the economic history of Britain since the war — that is, from the original Dunkirk spirit to the privations of the three-day week in the war between the Heath government and the miners. Five actors cut from 'illustrated lectures' to a variety of games with symbolic props to show in visual terms the causes of 'national decline' and the conflicting points of view of government, management, and workers. 'Surplus value' is represented by balloons, productivity agreements by a television game of chance with the dice loaded against the worker-contestants, international trade as a game of brag in which the winners can't let the losers drop out of the game, and Heath's politics of confrontation as an army being ordered to turn its rifles back-to-front. A variety of 'visual aids' enlivens the more straightforward episodes and make the statistics more digestible, but the play still makes considerable intellectual demands.

We rejected strict chronology. We still related to contemporary events and still used fact extensively, but this time we went back to 1945, the earliest point at which we felt we could start, to try and get an overview. We also felt the need to incorporate some images of basic principles — the labour theory of value and the surplus value concept. The show became, quite simply, too big, too complicated for the environments it was intended for.

Edgar, 'Return to Base', *New Edinburgh Review*,
No. 30 (Aug. 1975), p. 2-3

The agitprop play with which I am most pleased, because in two hours you actually get through the most massive amount of extremely complex material.

Edgar, 'Towards a Theatre of Dynamic Ambiguities', p. 8

The All-Singing, All-Talking Golden Oldie Rock Revival Ho Chi Minh Peace Love and Revolution Show

Musical extravaganza in three acts.
First production: Bingley College of Education, Mar. 1974.
Unpublished.

Written for a cast of 50 in two studio spaces between which the audience moves. The story of rock culture from the 'fifties to the 'seventies, through teds, mods, rockers, hippies, yippies, hell's angels, skinheads, and teeny boppers, taking in sex, drugs, politics, mysticism, and violence on the way.

Man Only Dines

A play in two acts, with music.
First production: Leeds Polytechnic, June 1974.
Unpublished.

Commissioned for the hundredth anniversary of the Yorkshire Training School of Cookery. Concerns a day in the life of a Victorian family, dealing with attitudes to etiquette, croquet, marriage, sex, feminism — and food. A high spot is the making of Mrs. Beeton's plum pudding recipe, with 36 eggs, onstage

I Know What I Meant

Television documentary, 45 minutes.
Television production: Granada, 10 July 1974 (dir. Jack Gold; with Nicol Williamson as Nixon).
Unpublished.

The forty hours of White House tape transcripts, involving

President Nixon, John Dean, Haldeman, Ehrlichman, and Ron Ziegler, edited by Edgar.

I can, perhaps, lay claim to having been the writer of the purest drama-documentary ever written, because, in 1974, during the Watergate crisis, I edited the White House tape transcripts into a 45-minute television play, in which every word spoken on screen had been actually spoken in reality, and we had the transcripts to prove it. But, in fact, of course, the play was bristling with impurities: the whole process of making it had consisted of value judgements, from my judgements about what to put in and leave out, to the director's judgements about what to look at, and the actors' judgements about pace and inflection and gesture and mood. And those judgements — about how the words were said, and why, and with what relative significance — added up to an argument, which was that Richard Nixon was progressively deluding himself about what he was doing, and that when he said he didn't know things that he did know, he wasn't pretending but concealing the memory from himself. . . . I'm sure that our act of turning those documents into drama, of showing one way in which those words *could* have been spoken by real human beings, had the effect of deepening our audience's understanding of those extraordinary events.

Edgar, 'On Drama-Documentary',
reprinted in *The Second Time as Farce*, p. 62-3

Like so much of Watergate itself, a dramatic comedy on the use and abuse of language. 'You've got to go through the whole place wholesale.' 'You mean *fire the whole staff?*' 'That's right.' Not one of the five conversationalists in the Oval Room is capable of saying anything out straight first time; it is not simply that they are being devious but rather that they are not entirely articulate. . . . This was not a cartoon, although it was very funny. Nicol Williamson occasionally permitted his upper lip to draw back over his teeth in an involuntary snarl and used his hands as if trying to push down a volcano but he was not giving an impersonation of the President. It was a beautifully even performance of a bullet-eyed leader literally sweating it out.

Michael Ratcliffe, *The Times*, 11 July 1974

O Fair Jerusalem

A play in three acts.

First production: Birmingham Repertory Th. Studio, May 1975
(dir. Christopher Honer).
Published: in *Plays: One.*

The main action occurs in 1348, when the Black Death reached England: other scenes are set in 1948, during rehearsals in a partially bombed church for a play which, it emerges, is the one we are witnessing. Judged as a 'metatheatrical' work, the piece is extremely complex, stylistically and structurally, and the 1348 action itself catches up a troupe of actors who duly perform plays within the play within the play. Elements of church ceremony and narrative-links add further complexity to the 'levels' of the action. Thematically, however, the through-line is clear: the pandemic of the plague in 1348 exerts pressures for social reform which lessen with the abatement of the disease and the restoration of order; but while all known pandemics could by 1948 be cured, the new scourge of the nuclear bomb is not so readily eradicated. The threat of war can, however, be overcome: 'It's not till now we've had the tools to do it'. The dense fabric of action and characterization prevents this message from appearing oversimplified, and a rich variety of linguistic styles — from pseudo-Chaucerian verse for the nobles, fluent doggerel for the players, earthy prose for the working people, and rich rhetoric for the religious fanatics — varies the tone of this lengthy play, as the range of action and characterization varies its pace. A number of characters recur — William, a wandering freed man; Ham, eventually sole survivor among the players, who goes mad; a Lady pregnant by a knight for whom she searches after the death of her Lord; Diccon, a mercenary longbowman; and John, a voice crying in the wilderness for the rights of the people.

That was a kind of attack on . . . fashionable despair. The point of the play was to say: no, it is not true that we live in an eternal cycle of ghastliness and that there is no way out. . . . Fireworks of construction perhaps conceal a slightly simplistic attitude to the moral, which works against itself in both ways. It means that the moral is not worked out, because there isn't time to work it out in enough detail to make it not simplistic, and that the fireworks conceal what the moral is, anyway. . . .

35

O Fair Jerusalem is really more of an allegory. The point it makes is that there are two views of the way in which great disasters always repeat themselves, and the way that human beings cope with those great disasters — which is, in Jan Kott's phrase 'like a mole'. One view is that of the mole who is scrabbling to the surface, but who knows he'll never reach it because the earth keeps falling in on him: that is the tragic mole, as opposed to the mole with the socialist view of history, who, however distant the light at the end of the tunnel, knows he is going to get there. . . . *O Fair Jerusalem* was an attempt to look at those two views of human history through two coincidentally related events, which happen to have occurred six hundred years apart — the foundation of the National Health Service, which is in a sense the enduring symbol of the hope represented by the election of a Labour Government at the end of the Second World War; and the Black Death, in which, in a highly superstitious and hierarchical society, a third of Europe was wiped out. . . .

Formally, the play was an attempt to accommodate a large cast in a small theatre. I wanted to do something environmental, spectacular, and I was offered a bit more on my budget than I usually had at the time. And I hadn't written a history play before, a play set in the far past. . . .

I got too concerned with the interesting technical problem of attempting to represent a society 630 years ago. I wanted to avoid 'M'lords' and 'prithees', or silly contemporary English, or what one would call 'neutral English' . . . so I just got fascinated by those technical problems.

Edgar, 'Towards a Theatre of Dynamic Ambiguities', p. 10-11

The style: severely Brechtian and rather boring. Actors forbidden any sustained identity: every scene cut short before we start to care, lots of black-outs with a fresh focus of attention. . . . The story teller's art was in abeyance that night: nothing to catch and inflame the spectator's imagination; though, as usual, there was something for his political conscience.

Eric Shorter, 'Regions', *Drama*, Autumn 1975, p. 66-8

Gradually his theme unfolds. The medieval world was slaughtered by the plague, and the plague has been cured. How it is cured is explained by a doctor called in for the purpose, though the details he gives are rather sketchy. But in the modern world there is another plague: war. I think that Mr. Edgar says that that can be cured too, but I am not sure. What is certain is that Mr. Edgar's progressive thinking is of the simple kind which lends itself easily to effective theatre. . . . Robert

O'Mahoney's delivery of the tirade against nuclear weapons is electrifying; the discovery of signs of plague on the legs of the girl tumbler and the quarrel between author and player are admirable scenes.

Harold Hobson, *Sunday Times*, 25 May 1975, p. 29

Censors

Play for television, 30 minutes, written in collaboration with Robert Muller and Hugh Whitemore.
Television production: 'Eleventh Hour', BBC, June 1975.
Unpublished.

A jury reveals its attitudes to sex and politics, and both together, in its arguments over a prosecuted dirty magazine.

Blood Sports

Five sketches, forming a play in two acts.
First production: of three of the scenes, entitled *Summer Sports*, Birmingham Arts Lab., 3 July 1975 (dir. David Edgar).
First London production: of *Summer Sports*, Bankside Globe, 7 Aug. 1975 (dir. Michael Waring); of *Blood Sports*, 28 June 1976 (dir. Dusty Hughes; with Simon Callow as Oliver, Jack, Shot-Putter, and Rider).
Revival: of *Ball Boys* (Scene i of Act I and all Act II of *Blood Sports*), Half Moon, ICA, and Battersea Arts Centre, London, June 1977 (dir. Noel Greig).
First American production: New Directors' Project, Perry St. Th., New York, 18 Nov. 1987 (dir. Judy Dennis).
Published: Ball Boys (London; Pluto, 1978); *Blood Sports*, complete, in *Shorts* (London: Nick Hern Books, 1989); *Ball Boys*, in *The Best Short Plays 1982*, ed. Ramon Delgado (Radnor, Pa.: Chilton, 1982), p. 28-44.

A series of comments on sports and sportsmen. Beaters *concerns two beaters on a grouse moor, the younger of whom is converted to Marxism by a copy of* Socialist Worker *he finds*

*wrapping his lunch and comes to a sticky end at the hands of the
gun-happy Bane of Froth. In* Cricket, *two incompatible fielders
communicate via a spectator on the boundary, play chess, and
discuss the State of the Nation. In the third sketch,* Shotputter,
*the tribal hero plans (and mis-executes) the murder of a 5,000-
metre champion; and in* Cross Country *a two-man proletarian
panto-horse breaks its leg and is shot by the foul-mouthed lady
rider. The second half of the play consists of* Ball Boys, *in
which two ball boys at the Wimbledon tennis tournament discuss
their menial roles on court. One-Eye has been sent off in
disgrace for breaking the lucky racket of the Swedish idol, Sven
Svenson, whose taped monologue — a stream-of-consciousness
meditation on women, ice, and blood — has opened the play.
They talk about the ethics of tennis and of revolution, and play
darts using a board decorated with Svenson's face. When the
star enters, pursued by his fans, the two boys murder him grue-
somely with a piece of cat-gut. The true revolution, One-Eye
declares, will be the uprising of 'the maimed, deformed, and
corpulent; the ugly, hare-lipped, and incontinent', against all
the beautiful and fashionable people of the world.*

Ball Boys is an attempt, through the story of two unlovely orphans in a
tennis club locker-room, to expose the essential contradictions inherent
in late monopoly capitalism, to analyze the role of neo-colonialism in
confirming the repressively-tolerant ideological interface between
superstructure and base (while remaining not unmindful of the need to
be fully cognizant of the essential dualism of the decaying bourgeois
apparatus), to express implacable hostility to the running dogs of craven
reformism in the labour bureaucracies, and to stress the vital need for
alternative modes of leadership to pose the essential question of state
power. It is arguable that in this project the play is not totally successful.

Edgar, *Ball Boys* (Pluto, 1978), p. v

This witty, often virulent quintet of plays is not about sport at all, but
about the divisions between people which sport exaggerates. . . . The
mutinous Wimbledon ball-boys prophesy the day when 'the bald and
warty shall seek and destroy the objects of their fantasies'; but their
horrible psychological truth is spoiled when, after the murder, one of
them questions whether they got it wrong. Edgar doesn't seem too
sure whether it's class or some deeper division in the collective soul that

he wishes to explore, and he sometimes mixes his thoughts rather clumsily.

Victoria Radin, *The Observer*, 4 July 1976, p. 22

The Midas Connection

Play for television, 30 minutes.
Television production: 'Eleventh Hour', BBC, 2 Aug. 1975 (dir. Mike Newell).
Published: in *Shorts* (London: Nick Hern Books, 1989).

Starts and finishes during the bizarre ritual of the twice-daily gold price fix in the City of London. Most of the play is about three workmen in a vault who spend the night shifting gold from one basket to another. They are visited by a young financial whizz-kid and his girl friend, who are anxious about the state of world markets: finally they panic.

The idea quickly wore thin, the development was far from zany enough, and would have probably benefited from more time to work on it.

Peter Ransley, *The Listener*, 7 Aug. 1975, p. 181

The National Theatre

A play in one act.
First production: Open Space, London, Oct. 1975 (dir. Peter Stevenson).
Published: in *Shorts* (London: Nick Hern Books, 1989).

It is set in a dressing-room occupied by three actresses who are appearing in a lunch-time show. The first to arrive is Ella (Katharine Schofield) who works through some lines from Three Sisters. . . . *As the second girl, Marie, arrives, and as Ella changes into a very un-Chekhovian costume, it gradually emerges that they are strippers in a club. But there is a deliberate, disillusioned parallel with* Three Sisters — *the prop-*

rietor, Alex, who directs his own shows, is known as the Colonel
— while the function of the play's title is not merely to mislead.
It is also a pointer to the main point of the play, which is that the
louche voyeurism the place caters for is characteristic of the
impotent consumerism rife in Harold Wilson's Britain. . . . Most
of it is written on a much more personal level, and the three
girls are deftly characterized. Ella is a failed actress who still
does voice exercises, and still entertains fantasies about suc-
ceeding. Her behaviour still accords with her middle-class
accent, and she still puts on an act of not really being middle-
class. Lynda Marchal gives an exuberantly and entertainingly
boisterous performance as Marie, a working-class girl who has
been having an affair with the Colonel, unaware of his
preference for another girl-friend, while Lindsay Ingram plays
Eileen, another working-class girl, who arrives late with
embarrassing bruises all over her body, having been raped by
her husband the night before. Considerable tension is generated
out of her predicament. . . . There is friction when Marie insists
on listening to the news over her transistor radio; there is a rich
mixture of rivalry and sympathy between the three of them, and
there is solidarity when Alex or the factotum invades their
territory. And there is a good climax when Marie and Eileen are
both sacked. Ella is kept on because she has a classy accent.

Randall Craig, 'Experimental', *Drama*, Winter 1975, p. 76

Events Following the Closure of a Motorcycle Factory

A play in two acts.
First production: Birmingham Repertory Th. Studio, Feb. 1976.
Unpublished.

A documentary history of the work-in which followed the
threatened closure of the Norton-Villers-Triumph motorcycle
factory at Meriden in 1973, which resulted in government
backing for the establishment of the Meriden Motorcycle
Co-operative there in the following year. The action develops in

the form of a many-levelled debate on the changing situation, utilizing contemporary documentation, invented dialogue, and musical interruptions, but few of the stylized confrontations or 'illustration games' of Edgar's earlier documentary plays. A straightforward, closely specific work, depending on mood rather than style changes to sustain its momentum.

Saigon Rose

A play in three acts.
First production: Traverse Th., Edinburgh, 8 July 1976 (dir. Chris Parr).
First New York production: Westside Mainstage, 26 Nov. 1982 (dir. Ted Davis).
Radio production: BBC Radio 3, 3 Apr. 1979 (dir. Michael Rolfe; with Alison Steadman as Vicky, Mirian Margolyes as Heather, Bill Paterson as McLusky, and Patti Love as Mo).
Published: in *Plays: One.*

Saigon Rose is a particularly virulent and resistant strain of gonorrhoea, mutated during the American involvement in Vietnam. Claymore, an American draft-resister, gives it to Vicky, a girl he meets and sleeps with in Edinburgh. She passes it on to her husband, Clive, before deciding to leave him; and he gives it to Mo, a waitress he picks up on the rebound, and who becomes a model for Claymore. This circular pattern of relationships is developed in the first half of the play, during which the disease is not mentioned, except elliptically in the solo-spots performed by Heather between scenes, in a variety of pulp-fiction idioms. Heather turns out to be the social worker responsible for tracking down all Claymore's sexual contacts, and in the final act is invited to a party at Clive's, together with McCluskey, Clive's best friend, and all the victims of Saigon Rose. The curtain falls on Mo and Claymore dancing, 'very slowly and beautifully'. Slightly plotted for Edgar, the play is fleshed out by the characterization of (in particular) Clive, a self-observing 'sixties radical, and his dependences — on Vicky, on Mo, and on the wry Marxist McClusky. An ironic celebration of the sourer fruits of permissiveness — and North Sea oil.

Sooner or later, somebody was bound to write a comedy about VD, sending up the clinical procedures and all, with even the doctor heartily trying to pretend that all is normal. . . . It is comedy with the strictly moral undertones not unfamiliar in the rising generation. . . . Only for the would-be worldly little Mo, whose bewilderment momentarily shows, and for Clive's bluff cynical friend, the Marxist Clydesider McClusky, who doggedly remains outside the circle, does the author allow us to feel sympathy even while we laugh.

Cordelia Oliver, *The Guardian*, 10 July 1976

The Perils of Bardfrod

Revue, written in collaboration with Richard Crane.
First production: opening production at Th. in the Mill, Bradford University, Nov. 1976.
Unpublished.

Questions the purpose of the new technological universities.

Wreckers

A play in two acts, with songs.
First production: by 7:84 Co. England, Barnfield Th., Exeter, 10 Feb. 1977, touring, including Half Moon Th., London, 19 Apr. 1977 (dir. Penny Cherns).
Published: Eyre Methuen, 1977.

The first half documents how in 1972 five dockers were jailed for picketing and released through union protests. Alternating with the progress of the struggle in the docks is a story of the capture and jailing of a little man dealing in stolen denim, while the police remain unconcerned with catching his bosses. The second half alludes to the failure of the Labour government to pass its Dock Labour Bill in an effective form, but concentrates on some of the same characters in 1976 — left-wingers in a local Labour Party trying to remove their right-wing Labour

MP, and replace him with someone more sympathetic. The parallels with Reginald Prentice's experiences in Newham in 1975 are often close.

Wreckers looks at the dominant radical tradition of the deviancy school — the idea, for example, that the Kray twins were somehow articulating an ill-formed but real protest against the capitalist system. So the set of ideas I wanted to confront and worry in *Wreckers* had to do with the fact that working-class life in the East End of London is based on an infrastructure of crime — which seemed to me the kind of question which revolutionary organs discussing the dock strike were unable to confront. That play was an attempt to look at criminality and actually ask, 'look, what is our attitude to theft? Do we actually believe that there are forms of anti-social behaviour which occur among working-class people which are directed superficially against the rich, but which are totally unacceptable?'

> Edgar, 'Towards a Theatre of Dynamic Ambiguities', p. 17

This show began with lengthy discussions between the group, the director Penny Cherns, and me. There was a strong feeling that the show should be about the law, both in its application and basic character. Out of this came the idea of a play set in the London Docks, which would deal with criminal law, with industrial law, and finally with the nature of parliamentary legislation as a whole. Having decided on the subject and agreed an outline, we researched the show, everyone reading around the subject, and conducting interviews collectively. . . . At the end of the research period, I produced another outline, which was discussed and amended. I then went away to write the script, returning some weeks later with a draft, which was extensively re-written during its five-week rehearsal.

> Edgar, 'Introduction', *Wreckers*, p. v

Despite the blatancy of its form, the play has subtleties and is richly entertaining. The 7:84 company have refined the use of music as an accusatory and unifying device which, given Mr. Edgar's pungent lyrics, keeps the show moving rapidly and keeps one involved in both the story telling and the politics.

> Ned Chaillet, *The Times*, 21 Apr. 1977

Wreckers has the feel of something written in committee. . . . The questions under discussion are: the Dock Labour Scheme and its scuttling by two absent MP's, the dock strike and arrests of 1972, the cut-rate machinations of the East End rag trade, the leaning bias of the police towards the dockers, squatting and the new Criminal Trespass Bill, the corrupt press, the attempt by left-wing militants to use the machinery of the Labour Party to unseat right-wing dissentients and being ruled unconstitutional for following the letter of the rule book. Not exactly a list of side issues. *Wreckers* tackles all these major questions and still has time for songs and music. It all makes for a rather crowded and confused evening. At odd moments *Wreckers* provides some real insights into the militant point of view and Edgar's ability to provide both sides with realistic punchy dialogue is evident, but in short snatches.

Allen Saddler, *Plays and Players*, Apr. 1977, p. 39

Ecclesiastes

A play for radio: 55 minutes.
Radio production: BBC Radio 4, 1 Apr. 1977 (dir. Michael Rolfe).
Published: in *Plays: Two*.

John Hammond, a Marxist vicar, radicalized by a visit to Bolivia, has chosen to work in the poorest parish south of the Trent. He hears that he may be a candidate for bishop, but he will of course turn it down, fearing the compromises this will impose on him. His son, Luke, a heroin addict, returns from America a Jesus freak, and confronts his father publicly. Hammond's embarrassment at this reveals to the establishment that he is the right choice for vicar. A year later he is preaching, moderately, that 'oppressors, too, have souls'.

Much of John Hammond's theology is based on a book I read by a then relatively unknown Anglican academic called David Jenkins.

Edgar, 'Introduction', *Plays: Two*, p. xiii

Destiny

A play in three acts.

First production: Royal Shakespeare Company, The Other Place, Stratford-upon-Avon, 22 Sept. 1976 (dir. Ron Daniels; with Ian McDiarmid as Turner, Michael Pennington as Rolfe, Bob Peck as Cleaver, and Cherie Lunghi as Liz and Carol).
First London production: Aldwych Th., 12 May 1977, trans. of Stratford production.
Revived: Half Moon Th., London, 11 July 1985 (dir. Chris Bond).
Television production: 'Play for Today', BBC-1, 31 Jan. 1978 (dir. Mike Newell; with Colin Jeavons as Turner, Nigel Hawthorne as Rolfe, and Iain Cuthbertson as Cleaver).
Published: Methuen,1976; revised, Methuen, 1978; and in *Plays: One*.

Edgar's new play spans two continents and nearly thirty years, from 1947 to the present day. There are several interlocking stories. The central action traces the odyssey of a provincial racist, one Sergeant Turner, who served with the army in India. Returned to England and civilian life, he opens a small antique business in a manufacturing town in the West Midlands, but is outraged to discover that the block of which his shop is part has been acquired by an Asian property company. Finding that his grievance awakens a sympathetic response within his small circle, he founds the Taddley Patriotic League — at first little more than a one-man protest movement, but which is absorbed into the neo-fascist National Forward Party. Turner is adopted as their candidate in a parliamentary by-election and polls quite a respectable proportion of the vote, but is utterly disoriented by the discovery that the wealthy businessmen funding National Forward are the real owners of the property company that caused all the trouble in the first place.

Turner's story is only one of many. We also follow the development of Major Rolfe, a Powell-like figure on the extreme right, who returns from India bitterly disillusioned by the loss of Britain's imperial role and what he sees as the ever-slackening fibre of our national life. His son is killed on active service in Ulster — a fact Rolfe blames on the spinelessness of the politicians at Westminster, and he becomes increasingly invol-ved in plans with like-minded army officers for a right-wing coup to get the country back on its feet again. We are shown the effect of creeping racialism on relationships between workers on the shop floor and the reluctance of the local Labour Party to take a principled stand on an issue running counter to the prejudices of many potential voters. There is also a series of hilarious and sharply written scenes describing the inter-factional disputes within the National Forward movement itself between the older members, intent on blaming everything on an international Jewish conspiracy, and the 'young lions', who insist that it's the blacks that are at fault. . . . The sheer breadth of the play's scope is itself exhilarating and it's packed with telling social detail. Particularly enjoyable is an episode in which the Taddley Patriotic League, all three of them, become affiliated to the Nation Forward Movement — the half-baked earnestness of the beleaguered little group is funny, night-marish, and entirely credible. . . . A part of Edgar's strategy as a dramatist is to shock his audience into awareness by the uncanny accuracy of his predictions. This is the true function of the detail with which each scene is crammed.

John Burgess, *Plays and Players*, Dec. 1976, p. 38

The play began as an idea in the wake of the Ugandan Asians crisis, when it seemed to me that the leadership of the anti-immigration movement was passing from people like Powell towards people who saw immigration as an issue to attract people to the extreme right. . . . I was determined from the start to show how the British middle class was just as susceptible to fascism, potentially, as the German middle class had been in the 1930s. And I drew a lot on my own background, and the fears and despairs of the British middle class. . . .

The play itself was based on detailed research into the extreme right. I'm now onto my seventh box-file of material, and I read about thirty books about contemporary and historical fascism, and interviewed about as many people, including a number of Asian and trade union leaders and other people involved in the struggle against fascism. Although the play is fiction — there are no real people in it, and the far-right groups are not real ones — every incident in it, with one exception, has happened, though not necessarily in that order. . . . There is a strike by Asian workers at a foundry in the play. Now here the actual progress of the strike is based on what happened at Mansfield Hosiery and Imperial Typewriters, while the atmosphere is based much more on the different conditions of the West Midlands foundry industry, and the struggles they've had there.

Edgar, 'Exit Fascism, Stage Right',
The Leveller, No. 6 (June 1977), p. 22

I hope it puts the frighteners on the conventional play-going audience — people who might be attracted in the direction of fascism — and I hope the play, which puts across a fairly controversial political line, will contain some political insights for the Labour movement audience. If *Destiny* has a virtue, it is that it is true. . . . There are a number of things about fascism which people now, thank God, do understand. They understand that it won't go away if you ignore it; they understand the kind of soil in which it flourishes. What I think they don't understand is why large numbers of ordinary people, often people heavily involved with the Labour movement, become attracted to an ideology which is self-evidently obscene. I wanted to create characters that the audience could relate to and in a way that they could confront in themselves. It is facile to say that all members of the National Front wander about in jackboots sieg-heiling all the time, that they are self-evidently ghastly horrible people. It is not only facile, it is counter-productive to create monsters (though there are some monsters in those parties). I wanted to create believable people. Some of them are pleasant; some of them are unpleasant.

Edgar, quoted in Catherine Itzin,
'Theatre, Politics, and the Working Class', *Tribune*, 22 Apr. 1977

The technique in *Destiny* I've rather uglily described as 'thematic linking', which is to say that a scene is followed by one which took place seven years earlier, followed by another which took place two years before that: not because I was flashing back, in the conventional sense, but because the answer to the question Scene C has posed took place seven years before, and *that* was Scene D, and the answer to the question Scene D posed came two years before that, and the answer to the question Scene E posed requires us to return to the present tense. What I wanted the audience to do was actually view the play in terms of its theme. . . .

Destiny had more effect, by virtue of being done at the Aldwych, than anything else I've written. Partly because it's better than a lot of what I've written, but partly because it became an event. And I would argue that its performance at the Aldwych had more effect than its production on television, despite the fact that it was seen by four million people on television and by twenty-two thousand at the Aldwych.

Edgar, 'Towards a Theatre of Dynamic Ambiguities', p. 12, 15

Destiny is an irritating play. It tells how the National Front (disguised, not *quite* impenetrably, as Nation Forward) is about to take over the country with the support of the army and the wicked capitalists, largely because the hero (a left-wing Labour candidate whose chief — indeed only — qualifications are his hatred of Roy Jenkins and his support of unrestricted Commonwealth immigration) sells out at the last moment, his sell-out consisting of his refusal to support breaches of the criminal law committed with a view to making the world safe for Trotskocracy. Then why do I not simply throw the programme into the wastepaper-basket and go to bed? Because much of the writing (by no means all, for some of it is as flabbily conformist and lazy as the substance) is so acute and convincing that there can be no doubt of Mr. Edgar's talent.

Bernard Levin, *Sunday Times*, 5 June 1977

In exposing a group that thrives on finding scapegoats for Britain's decline, it comes close to adopting that tactic itself. For all its documentary qualities, it is a hate-filled piece.

Irving Wardle, *The Times*, 29 Sept. 1976

A play which astonished me with its intelligence, density, sympathy, and finely controlled anger. For once, too, the compassion was not withheld from those deemed beyond the pale. Here was an examination of the extreme right in British politics which caught up all the strands which make it function: the nostalgia, the disappointment, the dumbly aching resentments, as well as the psychotic anti-semitism and other such racism that traditionally disfigures these movements.

Dennis Potter, 'A Play Astonishing in Its Excellence',
5 Feb. 1978, p. 35

It is, most importantly, the panoramic political play that writers of Mr. Edgar's generation have been straining after for years. Often they have strained too hard; Howard Brenton (in the last major contender, *Weapons of Happiness*) was a poet trying to turn himself into a journalist. Mr. Edgar has actually been a journalist and his play is, among other things, excellent reportage. . . . For once Marxism has inspired a playwright to generosity. Keeping his exploiters for the most part off-stage, Mr. Edgar is able to see all his characters as victims: a limiting vision if he were writing tragedy, but liberating here. Sure of his own position, he can take time to understand everyone else's. Even the aspirant Hitler of Nation Forward has a biting speech (delivered with uncomfortable rasping power by Bob Peck) about the fears of an old man surrounded by immigrants.

Robert Cushman, 'Further Thoughts on the RSC's Fascists',
The Observer, 22 May 1977, p. 30

Here was a project I have often imagined but never hoped to see: a strong and committed left-winger able to understand and to dramatize empathetically the psychology and doctrine of fascism; and, indeed, its working-class as well as its elitist appeal. Borkenau, Koestler, Orwell, and Silone argued the need to know the other side's feelings and case as well as one's own — advice seldom taken today. David Edgar, however, has produced a play about, on one level, a fascist intervention in a West Midlands by-election, on another about, of course, the retreat from empire and the risks of fascism today, almost wholly in terms of the nasties themselves. His clinical empathy is extraordinary. He does something so rare in the political theatre: he sends out the audience informed, disturbed, and thinking, not full of a surrogate glow of an evening's political passion. Types never seen on the stage in three dimensions before are now seen in their dens and at feeding time. He has a marvellous ear for language, and a well-controlled sense of the comic as seen in the ordinary. . . . The producer and the actors revel in their rich, difficult, and malicious tasks and do the author proud. A back-cloth of a military painting of a trooper cutting down a Sikh and baroque court music as scenes change, these remind us of both the brutality and the civilized pretensions of empire.

Bernard Crick, *Times Higher Education Supplement*,
20 May 1977, p. 11

There is something savagely funny about *Destiny*, just as there was something savagely funny about Brecht's *Arturo Ui*, and the two plays have something else in common: both were constructed as overt warnings of the rebirth of fascism, and yet both accept readily the feeble quality of its opposition. . . . What we have here is a high-class political thriller which ends with a predictable anti-fascist warning.

Sheridan Morley, *Shooting Stars* (London, 1983)

India, the link with the military, and the imperial hangover are given too much weight; the pathologies general to industrial capitalism are played down. . . . If *Destiny* were raunchier the correctness of its analysis would not matter so much. But most of the characters are made of sociological cardboard and they move gloomily along their historicist tramlines. . . . Significant it certainly is. Brecht it isn't.

John Turner, 'Facing the Front',
Times Literary Supplement, 2 Oct. 1985

The chill which the play sent through its first audiences as it illustrated the threat from a neo-Nazi movement is replaced in Chris Bond's production by the feeling that so much has happened since 1977 of more urgent interest at the polling booths — the miners' strike, for example. . . . The passage of time also diminishes the impact of a prognosticative drama which the author suggests in a programme note may not have lost its prophetic value in view of the 'slow crumble' of Thatcherism. Mr. Edgar is not Granville Barker. He cannot introduce into his ambitious politickers any feeling for dramatic character. It is the arguments which count, not the people.

Eric Shorter, *Daily Telegraph*, 15 July 1985, p. 10

Nine years after its first production by the RSC, David Edgar's panoramic but incisive study of the growth of a neo-fascist movement in Britain in the 1970s still seems not only one of the most impressive political plays that I have ever seen, but also horribly relevant to the general cast of events in the mid-1980s. . . . The virtues of Edgar's play are threefold. Cohesion, as well as a vital historical context, is provided by the way the narrative follows through the lives of three contrasting characters from the imperial twilight in India in 1947, to a by-election in the West Midlands twenty years later. . . . More striking still is Edgar's ability to reveal the range of motivations and insecurities that can lead people to support a national socialist movement. In addition, he succeeds in portraying the rifts and divisions among the established parties of the left and right with a vividness and conviction that never fails to impress.

Malcolm Hay, *Plays and Players*, Sept. 1985, p. 23

See also:
Martin Knelman, 'Inside Enoch Powell Country', *Saturday Night* (Toronto), XCII (Sept. 1977), p. 63-5.

Our Own People

A documentary play in two acts.
First production: by Pirate Jenny, touring, and at Half Moon Th., London, 30 Nov. 1977 (dir. Walter Donohue).
Published: with *Teendreams* (Methuen, 1987).

Edgar's new play is a 'Report of a Committee of Inquiry into the dispute between employees of the Darley Park Mills Limited and their employer.' . . . We first learn about the basic conflict. The Asian workforce (about half of the employees) of a small Yorkshire factory go out on strike, because they feel discriminated against concerning pay, promotion, and conditions of work. The strike committee is represented by three Asian workers. . . . The company is represented by Mr. Harper, Managing Director, and a barrister. The Inquiry is chaired by Baroness Cockburn, whose over-emphasized 'objectivity' is a rightly balanced caricature. Having built up the tension systematically, as in a good thriller, the second act (second day of Inquiry) offers a series of sad surprises. The corruptness of the company management and that of the union is exposed in its full complexity. We learn that one of the strike-leaders, who was excused from the Inquiry for some unspecified reason the previous day, has in fact been deported. . . . We also hear about an ambiguous deal, set up between management and union — 'It was not a formal, only a gentlemen's, agreement', as the senior steward puts it — concerning the transfer of modern weaving machines. The management is willing to deliver the new machinery, under the condition that no Asian workers are promoted to become 'time-weavers' (which is a much better paid and more responsible position). . . . Mrs. Dawson, the shop steward, loses her nerve and openly abuses the members of the strike committee at the Inquiry. . . . A young English working woman, neglected by her husband, pregnant, unpopular among her fellow-workers, mostly immigrant women, because of her racialist attitude, finds the only person in whom she can confide is a middle-aged woman, a member of the National Front. . . . It seems to be one of the major conclusions of this very significant play that without a multiracial, united workforce, working people will never be able to stop capitalistic manipulations and discriminations of sex and colour.

Ria Julian, *Plays and Players*,
Feb. 1978, p. 38

The Jail Diary of Albie Sachs

A play in two acts, based on the book of the same name (1966).

First production: Royal Shakespeare Company, Warehouse Th., London, 13 June 1978 (dir. Howard Davies; with Peter McEnery as Sachs), trans. to The Other Place, Stratford-upon-Avon, 11 Apr. 1979.

First American production: Manhattan Th. Club, New York, 18 Nov. 1979 (dir. Lynne Meadow; with Brian Murray as Sachs).

Revived: Young Vic, London, 6 June 1984 (dir. David Thacker; with Matthew Marsh as Sachs).

Television production: BBC-2, 23 Feb. 1981 (dir. Kevin Billingham; with Peter McEnery as Sachs).

Published: Rex Collings, 1982; revised, in *Plays: One.*

Sachs, a white lawyer, served two consecutive terms under the Ninety-Day Law in 1963 and steadfastly refused to answer questions. A couple of years later he was picked up again; times having advanced, he was subjected to sleep deprivation, and caved in after twenty-four hours. David Edgar's adaptation of Sachs's book is studiously anti-sensational; hence it concentrates on the first phase of his ordeal and gives a remarkably persuasive picture of the interior of a man's skull through six months of solitary. . . . Edgar, who has a flair for playing devil's advocate, gives him an Afrikaner keeper (himself in all senses a victim of prejudice) whose fumbling attempts at friendliness break through his own mental rigidity. (To keep our sympathy within bounds, the same actor, Edwin Richfield, later doubles as the notorious interrogator Swanepoel.)

Robert Cushman, *The Observer*, 25 June 1978, p. 24

[*Jail Diary*] sounds a worthy but off-putting read: what is theoretically duller than the story of a person locked up for months on his own? But in fact the book is never dull, indeed it is continuously riveting, because Albie Sachs brings to his story such clarity, such detailed perception, and such painful honesty about the personal, ideological, and moral dilemmas that faced him. The book is also — often and surprisingly — very funny. Albie Sachs is able, somehow, to look at his various captors — jailers and interrogators alike — with a keen, realistic, and even affectionate eye; an eye that reveals their humanness as well as their inhumanity; going a long way to explain how the man who wields the whip can smile while he is doing so. . . . It is an even colder world now than in 1963, and in that sense my stage adaptation of Albie Sachs's diary is a history play about South Africa. But I don't think it's a history play for England. I think it's a story that addressed itself, acutely, to this country's present. *Jail Diary* is a book about a person who discovers, painfully, that his rhetoric is real. It's about the ending of an age of political innocence, and the move into a different kind of world, in which the choices really matter, and therefore hurt a great deal more. And there are now many people in this country — good, radical people — who are finding that they too are speaking in a colder climate to a starker world.

Edgar, '*The Jail Diary of Albie Sachs*', in
The Warehouse: a Writer's Theatre, ed. Walter Donohue
(Dartington Theatre Papers, 3rd Series, 1979-80, No. 8), p. 13-14

[Edgar] was drawn to the material for three reasons, First, he says, he was drawn by the appeal of attempting to dramatize the subject of heroism. 'Since the war we have become very good at writing about forms of failure, angst, disillusionment. Heroism is a different matter. Albie is a man who, in a much more extreme way than will face anyone in Britain, has his beliefs on the line. But to a certain extent we can test the strength of our own commitment to our values and principles by looking at somebody in an extreme situation. Just as, if we are fathers, we're aided in our view of fatherhood by looking at the extreme circumstances of *King Lear*. The fact that all parents go through the experience of being rejected by their children is what makes it interesting and the extremity of the situation is what gives it its power and terror.'

He was also drawn by the desire to examine and understand the Afrikaner mentality — his play, *Destiny*, had earlier attempted to come to terms with alien attitudes in its depiction of a British Nazi party. 'I don't think on mainland Britain we have anything equivalent to the Afrikaner mentality, though I think it does have a lot in common with protestant grievances in Northern Ireland. In both cases you have the problem of a minority who feel they opened up a country and retain a view of themselves as an oppressed minority. You think, why can't the protestants be generous — they're top dog. But they don't view themselves as top dog!'

Fascinating to him, too, was the confrontation of two opposing views of the world, two philosophies of life, with apparently no common vocabulary of thought to bridge that gap. It is similar, he believes, to the widening gap between the right and left wing parties here. . . .

Edgar made contact with Sachs when he worked on the dramatization and Stephanie Sachs, Albie's wife, who herself spent time in jail, has advised on the television production. 'I was able to talk to him in 1977

53

for about three hours amid the bottles of his leaving party from the night before (Sachs is now in Mozambique), but I'm glad not to have known him well. He is a very strong character in the book and I wanted to write that character.' Sachs has since seen the play and read the text. 'He was very nervous and became — I think — less nervous. One or two things which I got wrong we changed for the book and for television.' . . .

'You could say it has an aggressive lack of sex! In the theatre I find we're going back to the early 'seventies, having to *justify* plays about public life, going right back to basic arguments.'

Henry Fenwick, 'An Arresting History',
Radio Times, 21 Feb. 1981, p. 16

Sachs himself, writing shortly afterwards, merely mentioned from time to time the uncertainty of ordinary policemen faced for the first time with their new political role, and the resentment of the uniformed branches of the security forces against the newly prestigious Special Branch. I wanted, writing many years afterwards, to give this much more prominence, and so selected, emphasized, and occasionally invented incidents to demonstrate these ironies. Also, I wanted to explore Sachs's internal ambivalence about his own heroism in resisting the authorities in a way that he, obviously, couldn't do in a book about himself. So, again, my selection was made with that in mind, and, again, I found new material, partly from external sources, and partly from my own imagination. The result, I think, was quite clearly a play by a person who was not concerned in the events of his play, about a book by a person who was.

Edgar, 'Adapting *Nickleby*', *The Second Time as Farce*, p. 146

Surely Sachs came nearer to disintegration, plumbed deeper into despair, than Edgar allows. Surely there are opportunities, even with the present script, for McEnery to make us share the horror of not knowing how many multiples of 90 he must endure alone. As it is, all is clenched endurance and gritty distress, not quite enough under the circumstances.

Benedict Nightingale, 'Lab-Rat', *New Statesman*,
23 June 1978, p. 858

The Jail Diary is close to a monologue. The diary is only, rudimentarily, dramatized, and does not appear to have gained appreciably in its transition from text to theatre.

Mel Gussow, *New York Times*,
19 Nov. 1979, Sec. III, p. 15

There is a documentary value to a play like David Edgar's *The Jail Diary of Albie Sachs* independent of any aesthetic qualities. And that is its function in disseminating information.

Catherine Itzin, *Tribune*, 7 July 1978, p. 12

One could take his story in several ways: as a pivotal moment in South African politics when apartheid began repressing whites as well as blacks; as an example of the impotence of liberalism in a revolutionary context; or as yet another example of the power of modern police methods to crush even the best men. Mr. Edgar touches on these and other themes, but it is far from clear what his play is about. For one thing, to see Sachs in political perspective we need to know much more about his politics. Was he an active supporter of the banned African National Congress? Whom had he defended in court? Was he in possession of secret information, or merely being persecuted for refusing to toe the line? Whatever the reticence of his own book, it is very surprising to find such omissions in the work of a writer as politically literate as Mr. Edgar. Having exchanged front-line British public themes for a past episode in another country, one would have expected him to justify the piece by strengthening its documentary precision and its links with the present. But in Howard Davies's production the play's main effect is to make you feel sorry for a nice man shut up in a cell. Why he is in there and why he refuses to speak the words that would secure his release do not amount to much theatrical importance. Even on sentimental terms, the play contains some contradictions. For instance, Sachs proclaims that it is brutal actions that he hates, not those who commit them; and he confirms this by striking up a tentative friendship with an ex-nazi station commander. But there is no confirmation of the 'even-jailers-are-human' theory in the trio of sneering sadists who pursue Sachs from cell to cell, handing him his release only to re-arrest him. Also, while Sachs is quite aware that he is getting it soft in comparison with the Africans, at the same time we see him kicking up a great fuss over trying to get his blankets changed and see a doctor. Technically the obvious problem is that of dramatizing the experience of solitary confinement.

Irving Wardle, 'Too Many Unanswered Questions', *The Times*, 18 June 1978

This thrilling piece of theatre is above all else about courage and survival, the emergency resources of mind and body which some rare people are able to call in aid in extreme times. . . . The nature of the play's concerns and factual origins help to give *The Jail Diary of Albie*

Sachs a quality of excitement and the capacity to make you care and feel beyond anything else now in London theatre.

Nicholas de Jongh, *The Guardian*, 18 June 1978

As Albie, Brian Murray gives a complex, munificent, subtly chiseled yet ultimately towering performance. This Albie is faintly fatuous even at his best; his defiance is humpbacked, his brave words a bit buffoonish. But Murray conveys intelligence in action: thoughts watching themselves being hatched and taking wing; the mind forced to be both performer and spectator and enjoying both. When he cannot pad a harsh, cement wall with sensuous bonhomie, he plays a kind of mental squash against the naked hardness. But when he cannot even play this squash, and squashes fists of flesh against metal doors, he makes us feel his physical defeat and pain as keenly as his intellectual victories. Particularly moving is the way he regresses — becomes more childish, clownish, sluggish as confinement corrodes him — and how, when he cannot bounce, he crawls back. The role (as long and arduous as Hamlet) demands nonstop physical and mental energy, which Murray rises to with superb pacing, shading, shaping.

John Simon, 'More than We Deserve', *New York*, 3 Dec. 1979, p. 109

Mary Barnes

A play in three acts, adapted from *Mary Barnes: Two Accounts of a Journey through Madness*, by Mary Barnes and Joseph Berke (1971).
First production: Birmingham Repertory Th. Studio, 31 Aug. 1978 (dir. Peter Farago; with Patti Love as Mary and Simon Callow as Eddie).
First London production: Royal Court Th., 10 Jan. 1979, trans. of Birmingham production.
First American production: Long Wharf Th., New Haven, 5 Mar. 1980 (dir. Arvin Brown; with Eileen Atkins as Mary).
Published: Eyre Methuen, 1979; revised, Methuen, 1984; and in *Plays: One*.

An account of the unorthodox but successful treatment of a schizophrenic woman, through love and personal contacts in a Laingian community. First diagnosed as a schizophrenic in 1950, Mary Barnes is 42 when she comes under Joseph Berke's

care in a rambling East End house in 1965. In this extended
family environment, she relives the traumas of her early life, and
is slowly transformed from a demanding, regressive, middle-
aged child into a responsive, caring member of her new
'family'. Mary's personal rebirth is counterpointed by an
account of the development of the therapeutic community itself
and of the 'alternative' radical psychiatry it practises, with all
its allegiances and antagonisms, within the context of the
political and social mood of the late 1960s.

Mary Barnes [the book] . . . is a true story, set in the recent past, about a
group of people who believed fiercely in a particular view of the nature
of madness, and who attempted to live that belief in a peculiarly intense
and passionate way. This has led to problems in adapting the book for
the stage. The first was that I needed to fictionalize the characters in the
book in order to give myself the freedom to represent their community
dramatically. . . . Second, the exigencies of time and clarity forced me to
telescope and even alter many of the events in the book, to combine
functions and people.

Edgar, 'Author's Note', Mary Barnes, p. 7

The play presents a kind of counterpoint, I hope, so that the audience
gets amused and perhaps irritated by the psychiatrist, but are confronted
with their own emotional response to Mary's story, to a point that I call
dynamic ambiguity which will hopefully lead to people's attempting to
resolve it in their own minds, as opposed to an unpositive ambiguity.

Edgar, 'Towards a Theatre of Dynamic Ambiguities', p. 9

I became fascinated by the way, in the late 1960s, that the conventional
divisions of human experience were broken down, and, in particular, in
the way in which the personal, the political, and the spiritual sides of life
were made to relate to each other in a way they hadn't related before.
Writing ten years on, I needed a metaphor to demonstrate this truth
which was, of course, an assumed fact of life at the time when the book
was written. So I decided to give each of the three acts — in all of which
the schizophrenic Mary Barnes goes through a process of psychic
disintegration and reassembly — a specific theme and character. The
first act was set within a psychological mode of reality: I was concerned
to show the challenge of the so-called 'anti-psychiatry' movement to the
conventional relationship of patient and doctor. The second act was

constructed round a religious metaphor: Mary Barnes's vision of her suffering as an imitation of Christ's death and resurrection. And the third act, in which Mary began to relate to other people again, was much more social in its flavour: the world outside, in the shape of hippies, Vietnam war protests and so on, intervened in the action for the first time.

Edgar, 'Adapting *Nickleby*', *The Second Time as Farce*, p. 145-6

[Cast as Joe Berke] I immediately went to meet Joe. He proved quite different to the narrator of the book as I'd imagined him. I'd expected a dynamic thrusting Californian figure in jeans. What I saw before me was much more interesting. . . . This man was professional, not an inspired hippy, but a rigorously analytical, highly organized intellectual. In time, I saw that this man was infinitely more interesting to play than the man I'd sloppily imagined. My visit to him had been a one-man Joint Stock workshop. . . .

Patti Love had already deeply immersed herself in Mary Barnes. On the first day, Mary herself came to Birmingham. She burst into the room in her flowing clothes, sought out Patti and cried: 'Mary!' The two women fell into each other's arms and spent the day together, painting great murals. Back in the rehearsal room, we were discussing with David Edgar what it all meant, the contending psychiatric theories, the attitude of East Enders to having a centre of schizophrenics on their back doorstep, how exactly the liberations of the 'sixties had come about. We talked through the play for four days, till everything was understood by everyone. In this way, we were all focused on the whole play all the time, and never on 'my part'. . . .

Mary Barnes is the only production I've been involved in which really followed the Strasberg path in its quest for total emotional reality, and Patti's performance is the only 'Method' performance I've acted with. It was exactly what was needed.

Simon Callow, *Being an Actor* (Methuen, 1984), p. 73-4

There are really two plays going on here. One — moving and fascinating, though not always easy to watch — depicts the re-habilitation of Mary, who steps on to the stage as a frenzied 40-year-old child (and soon regresses further), but leaves as an accomplished painter. . . . Mary lives and is treated in a 'therapeutic community', most of whose members just happen to be doctors. That at least is the theory; its practical complications are the subject of the second and less satisfactory play. There are usually five or six people in residence and — mostly when sitting around a candle-lit supper table — they argue. . . . The period is the late 1960s, and between them the communards — shrugging pragmatists or impatient spouters — sum up the counter culture (pop records fill in the gaps). I wouldn't put it past Mr. Edgar to bring this off, but he needs more room.

Robert Cushman, *The Observer*, 3 Sept. 1978, p. 23

This community (like that of the tent-builders in Storey's *The Contractor* or of the footballers in his *Changing Room*) rapidly acquires its own momentum and its own characters: there's the drop-out, the eccentric, the orthodox, and the rebel, each of them coming into some sort of contact with Mary and either staying or going as a result of that contact, until at the last it is Mary who has become the central upholder of the community that was originally gathered to save her.

Sheridan Morley, *Shooting Stars* (London, 1983), p. 167

Edgar is anxious that we see the shrinks as human, vulnerable and uncertain — anxious to make it clear that Mary is being accompanied on her journey, not simply pointed in the right direction and waved off. To this end, he has organized an effective counterpoint between their own nervous tension and occasional anger — coming at times when the extremity of Mary's behaviour transmits a defensive fury to one or more of them — and the casual, efficient, compassionate, and inventive manner in which they more usually cope with her blood-curdling, manic outbursts. During these latter passages, the doctors have about them the cool but dedicated air of people dealing with a situation familiar to them, but none the less dangerous for that. It's a nicely drawn point; but it does serve to illustrate what I took to be one of the play's major drawbacks. There is a distinct vaudeville aspect in madness: its postures, its indignities, its bizarre verbal connections. In life, and at close-quarters, such behavioural fractures are indescribably chilling. On stage, they tend to get laughs, indeed, they invariably *did* get laughs. . . .

A similar kind of fault lies in the play's attempts to present, in pursuit of its argument, too many examples, too episodically, over too long an evening. With the appearance of Angie, a middle-aged victim of maternal smothering, much of the tension drains away. As compensation, though — and in fairness — the introduction of Mary's brother, Simon, heralds a passage of considerable power. Simon is a man crushed by drugs, gripped by compulsion neuroses, and wrestling, it seems, with a sinister deference to his own affliction. . . . Mary, though, is the focal point: raving, sly, vicious, deluded, desperate, she rants and punches and wails her way through madness to a kind of health, painting the walls with her own excrement, having to be bottle-fed, dumping her hysterical anguish on anyone and everyone with brutal randomness. It's a demanding part — not least for being easily overdone. Patti Love takes it at full pitch most of the way, keening and shrieking in a demented voice that now and then weakens to admit a plaintive tone.

David Harsent, 'Open Nerves', *New Statesman*, 19 Jan. 1979

It is not always clear with what degree of sympathy or seriousness the author intends one to view his therapists. They are certainly not the 'nutters, layabouts, and perverts' execrated by their neighbours; but — perhaps worse in the theatre — they are pompous and boring. . . . I was surrounded by members of the trade, who not only whispered their recognition of real-life colleagues but chortled merrily. . . . It contains a number of compelling, if uncomfortable and even repellent, scenes.

Francis King, 'In Two Minds',
Sunday Telegraph, 14 Jan. 1979, p. 12

We came away from the play thinking more about Miss Barnes's sickness — a scene, for example, in which the character strips to the nude and covers her body with her own excrement — than about her eventual sanity. In contrast, Marsha Norman's *Getting Out* not only pictured a disturbed personality, it also moved us by dramatizing the causes and the effects of the disturbance. . . . For some theatregoers, the experience may seem too close and even oppressive. The play offers no solution, which may be the author's principal intention.

Mel Gussow, *New York Times*, 6 Mar. 1980, Sec. III, p. 21

See also:
Mark Bly, 'Theater in New Haven: the Strange Case of *Mary Barnes*', *Theater*, XI, No. 3 (Summer 1980), p. 104-7.

Teendreams

A play in 24 scenes (first version); 19 scenes (revised version), written in collaboration with Susan Todd.
First production: Monstrous Regiment, Van Dyck Th., Bristol, 25 Jan. 1979 (dir. Kate Crutchley; with Gillian Hanna as Frances), touring to Sheffield, Bradford, York, Bingley, Brighton, Birmingham, and ICA Th., London.
First production of the revised version: Van Dyck Th., Drama Dept., Bristol University, 11 Mar. 1987 (dir. Martin White).

First London production of revised version: Askelon Co., Chair Th.,
   Kensington Park Pub, Ladbroke Grove, 13 June 1988.
Published: Methuen Theatrescript, 1979; revised, with *Our Own People*
   (Methuen, 1987).

The play's centre is Frances, one of those left-wing, middle-class women drowning in guilt whom I've seen frequently on the stage but never in life. A veteran of the student movement of the 'sixties (where she discovered that the woman's place is at the duplicating machine), she now enjoys an occasional night with her former live-in lover — who is one of those Marxists who doesn't believe in 'small-group consciousness' like the women's movement. Frances now teaches in a London comprehensive, where one of her pupils, hung up on the idea of boys, tries to commit suicide. . . . Here he loses sight of his characters in a panorama which attempts to cover, in addition to Frances and the new generation, squatters, an oppressed mother of two, and an overweening headmaster (a devil who gets all the best tunes). The issue of equality for women is reduced to arguments about who does the washing-up; and all the play can offer in the way of hope is its final image of two women, finally shot of their men, going out on the town together.

Victoria Radin, 'Cuckolds at the Court',
The Observer, 4 Mar. 1979, p. 16

It was a play which had plainly come out of the workshop a trifle unfinished and a product of propaganda, not an artistic impulse. As such it seemed honest.

Eric Shorter, 'Regions', *Drama*, Spring 1979, p. 70

If it has a message, it is one of consolation to people disappointed that the revolution turns out not to be an overnight affair. . . . Occasionally the production by Kate Crutchley lapses into a crude and unsuccessful theatricality, notably with a disco scene (Bay City Roller vintage) which I thought patronized its subjects without properly illuminating the poverty of the diet provided for them by vapid music and horrendous 'romance' magazines.

Paul Allen, *Plays and Players*,
Mar. 1979, p. 28

The first half is certainly a dismal business, which confuses you with its chronological jumps and doubling-up of parts, and positively exasperates you with its refusal to come seriously to grips with a potentially interesting subject, the radical left's failure to concede that sexual equality may be a necessary precondition to social change. . . . Progress, it is admitted, won't be simple, won't be painless. There is even a debate of sorts about the perimeters of liberation in which a chary male view is put with some understanding.

Benedict Nightingale, 'Dirty Business',
New Statesman, 9 Mar. 1979, p. 340

Nicholas Nickleby

A play in two long parts: the first in two acts, the second in three acts.
First production: Royal Shakespeare Company, Aldwych Th., London,
6 June and 12 June 1980, revived 13 Nov. and 23 Apr. 1981
(dir. Trevor Nunn and John Caird; with Roger Rees as Nicholas,
David Threlfall as Smike, and John Woodvine as Ralph Nickleby).
First New York production: RSC production, Plymouth Th., 5 Oct.
1981.
Revived: Royal Shakespeare Th., Stratford-upon-Avon, 13 Dec. 1985,
touring to Newcastle, Manchester, Los Angeles, and New York
(dir. Nunn and Caird; with Michael Siberry as Nicholas and John
Lynch as Smike).
Television production: Channel Four, 7, 14, 21, 28 Nov. 1982.
Published: in *Plays: Two*; two vols., New York: Dramatists Play
Service, 1982.

Stage version of Charles Dickens's novel.

When we began, we had only one rule: we were going to adapt the whole of *Nicholas Nickleby*, or, at the very least, we were going to tell the whole story. . . . What the research we did on the 1830s demonstrated was that the technological revolution, and the social upheavals that followed from it, had created a world of unfathomable economic opportunity but also one assailed by bottomless social doubt.

Edgar, 'Adapting *Nickleby*', *The Second Time as Farce*, p. 149, 150

George Orwell saw, for instance, that Charles Dickens really wanted all the energy and mobility and challenge to outmoded hierarchies that followed on from industrialization; but he wanted those things without losing what had gone before, the fixed relationships of country life, the kindness and paternal support of feudalism. So hence, in *Nickleby*, he creates the brothers Cheeryble, capitalists with a feudal face, impossible philanthropists who dole out largesse to the needy with a gay abandon that in the real world would force their business into bankruptcy within an afternoon. And so, too, he creates the end, where our heroes and heroines are frozen by good fortune into an unending and unchanging state of pure contentment.

The point, we found, is not that Dickens was an idiot, or that he did not mean it, but that what he meant was a complexity of aspiration for the ideal, and regret for the impossibility of achieving it; and that this tells us a great deal about him and even more about the times he lived in. So, in dealing with these crucial passages, I tried to adapt the book in a way that revealed not only the material, but also the complexities and ambiguities of Dickens's attitude to it, and the complexities and ambiguities of our response to those as well.

In addition, we tried to represent these ambiguities with techniques other than those that have become, in the time since Dickens wrote, jaded, corny, and even, sometimes, risible. So we tried to make the complex moments complex, and the moving moments moving, by using our own theatrical language, by trying, as it were, to strip away the darkened varnish from the painting. And, paradoxically, I think that, by quite fundamental changes in a lot of scenes and sequences, our vision of what Dickens meant was closer to what he really meant than if we had just presented what he wrote; because we did it, just like Dickens, in the language of the present, but, unlike Dickens, with the changed perspectives of a century and a half of passing time.

Edgar, 'Recrystallization of the Novel',
The Times, 26 Nov. 1980, p. 9

I think the achievement of *Nicholas Nickleby*, if you like, in ideological terms is three fold. First of all, it looks at adaptations in a new way. It says that a group of people with a strong view about the world can take a work of art and frame it and transform it in a way that makes the adaptation one not *of* the original work of art, but *about* the original work of art. Point two is that it has proved to be a genuine piece of popular theatre. It's accessible; it's not obscure. It's art, it's highbrow stuff, and it's culture, but the response we've had has been a wonderful popular response. The third point is that it was the only show, with the possible exception of *Accidental Death of an Anarchist* [by Dario Fo], on in a large London theatre, which was on the side of the underdog for the entirety of its not inconsiderable length. It's a show which is highly ambivalent about riches, highly antagonistic towards moneymaking, in favour of schoolboys against schoolmasters, in favour of employees against employers, in many respects, in favour of actors against directors, in favour of women against men, and servants against masters.

The project was to fill a London theatre with a thousand sophisticated, cosmopolitan, cynical, laid-back, late-seventies, trendy people and make them cry, laugh, hiss, and boo. The key thing was to see that they burst into tears three times; that they were genuinely horrified, saddened, and catharized by the death of Ralph, Ralph Nickleby, the stage villain-uncle to end all stage villain-uncles. The most important thing to get right was the death of Smike. There's no question that one of the most satisfying moments on the first Saturday that we put the whole show together was to look behind you up in the dress circle and see little white flags of kleenex waving at you in surrender.

Edgar, 'Interview', in Elizabeth Swain,
David Edgar, Playwright and Politician, p. 330-1, 335-6

First of all, it was cheering to note that the 'seventies movement towards democratic collectivism in the theatre had not entirely run out of steam (it was to do so later in the decade); second, its length (both of preparation and performance) and its success (on both sides of the Atlantic) led it to dominate my life in a way I couldn't have predicted. But I believe also that its success owed much to the beginnings of something else: a feeling that if the urge towards egalitarianism and social justice had indeed lost its sap and vigour, then their cultural roots should be preserved and nurtured, against the day when they would put forward new buds and blossoms in the future. In that sense, *Nickleby* was an early — if not the first — shot in the war that was to dominate the cultural landscape in the later 'eighties, about the uses of history and heritage (in general) and the nature of Victorian values (in particular). The message of Dickens's novel and our adaptation — that material self-interest is neither the first nor the most effective motor of human behaviour — was clearly an attractive one, even to people who felt that taxation needed cutting and union bosses taming.

Edgar, 'Introduction', *Plays: Two*, p. xi-xii

'Adaptation' is a feeble word for the structural invention, tonal emphasis, and stylistic definition of David Edgar's text, and for its skill in re-creating the realities of 1838 from the vantage point of 1980.

Irving Wardle, 'A Joy We Don't Deserve',
The Times, 26 Nov. 1980

The Aldwych itself has been transformed by the designers, John Napier and Dermot Hayes, with a runway projecting into the stalls, a catwalk ringing the front of the dress-circle, and the stage itself occupied by two sloping bridges that meet in a central pillar. The wealth of railings, grilles, and ironmongery also suggests the harshness of 1830s England. . . . The production is very successful at achieving complex effects through simple means. The stage in which Nicholas and Squeers set off for Yorkshire is built up out of skips and tables placed on a central rostrum. The cabriolet from which Sir Mulberry Hawk is thrown is conjured up through a press of scrum-down bodies with a velvety black cloth suggesting a rearing horse. And, most effectively, the harsh and dismal London through which the villainous Ralph Nickleby finally flees is created by a knot of actors emitting 'a windy suspiration of forced breath' or simply standing in a fixed line with their backs turned towards him. . . . In a vast cast one can only briefly commend Roger Rees as a splendidly violent, sudden, impulsive Nicholas, Edward Petherbridge (the most Dickensian of the lot) as a Newman Noggs full of grizzled, dithering, long-ankled goodness, Suzanne Bertish for a gash-mouthed Fanny Squeers, and a fluting, tootin' Mrs. Snevellici.

Michael Billington, *The Guardian*, June 1980

What has to go [from Dickens's novel], irretrievably, is the insouciant asides ('two live Members of Parliament looking so pleasant that it seemed a perfect marvel how any man could have the heart to vote against them') that makes Dickens so literally irresistible a satirist. The loss is compounded by a certain native earnestness in the RSC production. Any pamphleteer could make people shudder at Dotheboys Hall (and many did); it took Dickens to make them laugh, and to get the Yorkshire schools closed down. If these scenes at the Aldwych are not horrific enough, the basic reason is that they are not funny enough. Squeers is a juicy character; Ben Kingsley, who plays him, is a dry actor. (He makes amends later as a drunken member of the Crummles troupe.) Then, what misplaced integrity caused John McEnery to play the imposter Mantalini, whose joke depends on exquisite affectation, as dead common? Melodrama is softened too.

Robert Cushman, 'Novel Epic', *The Observer*, 29 June 1980

The Dotheboys scenes lend themselves perfectly to the theatre and are well done; they provide the only moment in the whole of the two evenings which is seriously upsetting rather than sentimentally moving. The remainder of the first evening is theatrically a disaster; the Mantalini episodes are tiresomely unfunny — Kate Nickleby is such a pill, the

Kenwigs/Lillyvick sub-plot (of which there is more to come in Part Two) is lacking in all theatrical potential, and the Crummles episodes, although one of the most admired parts of the book, become too much of a self-regarding theatrical cliché when re-imported from the novel to the stage.

Peter Jenkins, The Spectator, 28 June 1980

[One is] so grateful for a theatre piece that tries to offer us a fully dimensioned social world that one feels ungracious caviling about the simplified nature of that world. And the actors bring so much belief to their parts, and so much gusto, that they almost have us believing the sentiment too. Part of the joy the audience experiences surely comes from those who perform the play, and perform it with such pleasure. This kind of material is guaranteed to stimulate an English actor's imagination because, along with being pre-Marxian, it is also pre-Freudian. The characters bear no burden of neurosis or internalization. Except for some mild passes by the aristocratic villains, they don't even seem to have any sexuality. . . . Thus, the pleasures one finally takes home from the evening are not just those of seeing a story told well, or watching a lively novel transferred vividly to the stage, or feeling our nodding social consciences awakened, but rather of witnessing a large and brilliant company working skilfully and tirelessly on a highly complicated project. We have seen these techniques of transformation employed before (in Paul Sills's *Story Theatre*) but never so ambitiously.

Robert Brustein, Who Needs Theatre?
(New York: Atlantic Monthly Press, 1987), p. 196-7

Edgar has not simply translated Dickens to the stage. He has actually seized on three of the novel's key motifs: money, London, and role-playing. And the greatest of these is money. It becomes the play's protagonist and is seen from shifting viewpoints: a dead and sterile thing when garnered by Ralph Nickleby or used to establish a trade monopoly by the Hot Muffin Company, a beneficent one when philanthropically dispensed by the Cheeryble Brothers or when employed by Nicholas to restore his family's Devonian home. Dickens does not offer (nor does Edgar) a Marxist condemnation of capital. Instead he paints a vivid picture of a society where wealth and poverty live side by side in obscene juxtaposition and where money is the source of both darkness and light. David Edgar brings out and even heightens the polarities within the book.

Michael Billington, The Guardian, Jan. 1986

[Nunn, as director of the television version] hit upon a solution sublime in its simplicity. A single set, virtually unadorned, serves as the eye for a surrounding hurricane, for a blizzard of ingenious blocking and intricate stage-mechanics that are cinematic in their emphasis on speed, on getting quickly out of one scene and into another. For example, two actors stand back to back, then gracefully revolve to signal a transition from the misery of a Yorkshire school to the hypocrisy of a London salon. Recognizing a kindred spirit, the camera revels in such a figurative 'dissolve'. Even more important is Nunn's much-celebrated device of 'collective narration'. The cast, sometimes individually, sometimes collectively, frequently step out of the first person and into the third. Thus Roger Rees, as Nicholas, will suddenly leave a 'dramatized' sequence, turn straight to us and claim of his just-vacated character: 'He felt a depression of heart and spirit which he had never experienced before.' Far from being off-putting or distracting, the effect is wonderfully liberating. Certainly, it frees writer David Edgar to plagiarize directly from Dickens not only dialogue but atmosphere and mood. Consequently, the book's 'interior' sections (those intrinsically novelistic passages that standard film adaptations either ignore or offer in pretentious 'voice-overs') are delivered hot from the page by the actors themselves, who begin to acquire the function and weight of a Greek chorus. Indeed, the entire ensemble doubles as the omniscient author. They're both the puppets and the puppet-master.

Rick Groen, 'Dickens Has No Cause for Complaint',
Toronto Globe and Mail, 12 Mar. 1983, Sec E, p. 3

See also:

John Caird, 'Dickens on Broadway', *Horizon*, Sept. 1981, p. 57-61. [Interview with the co-director.]

Steve Lawson, 'Broadway's Nine-Hour Spectacular', *Saturday Review*, Sept. 1981, p. 21-3.

Benedict Nightingale, 'How 42 Actors and Two Directors Assembled *Nicholas Nickleby*', *New York Times*, 4 Oct. 1981, Sec. II, p. 1, 6.

Michael Patterson, 'A Novel Way of Staging the Novel', *Studien zur Asthetik des Gegenwartstheaters*, ed. Christian W. Thomsen (Heidelberg: Carl Winter, 1985), p. 240-8.

Susan Raven, 'The Return of *Nicholas Nickleby*', *Sunday Times Magazine*, 9 Nov. 1980, p. 72-4.

Roger Rees, 'Delving for Dickens', *Royal Shakespeare Company 1980–81*, ed. Simon Trussler (Stratford: RSC Publications, 1981), p. 55-6. [Describes the company's research on the Victorian period.]

Leon Rubin, *The Nicholas Nickleby Story* (Heinemann, 1981). [Excellent full-length account.]

Maydays

A play in three acts.

First production: Royal Shakespeare Company, Barbican Th., London, 13 Oct. 1983 (dir. Ron Daniels; with Antony Sher as Glass, John Shrapnel as Crowther, Bob Peck as Lermontov, and Alison Steadman as Amanda).

Published: Methuen New Theatrescript, 1983.

Maydays *is exactly what the Barbican is for: a big public play on a big public theme. Its territory is nothing less than the map of post-war politics. But its achievement is that it unites the epic and the individual. . . . In three and one-half crowded hours, Edgar gives us a sense of the patterns of history, but he still manages to focus on the individual conscience. Indeed he concentrates on three very different defectors. Jeremy Crowther (suavely played by John Shrapnel) is the classic pre-war leftie who dreams of having been a red at Trinity, swims along with the tide of post-war socialism, and then does a volte-face when he sees the students of 1968 staging demos and sit-ins: he is the romantic revolutionary. His one-time pupil Martin Glass (an incisive Antony Sher) is a middle-class vicarage renegade who swallows the 'sixties revolutionary shibboleths, is drummed out of the Socialist Vanguard, and who swings round to become an enemy of the nanny-state: he is the misfit revolutionary. And behind them looms the figure of Pavel Lermontov (a majestic Bob Peck): the Soviet labour-camp dissident who comes to the West only to find that he is being appropriated by the new authoritarianism. One of Edgar's many achievements is to give us a rich sense of the ironies of history. He movingly shows us the bewilderment of an idealistic American father in the 'sixties confronting the vengefulness of his progeny. He starkly counterpoints the black humour of Soviet gulag with the lofty disdain of a cosseted renegade like Crowther. He shows the young Martin Glass suffering political remorse at a boozy 'seventies party. . . . It has the inestimable advantage of a huge, hangar-like set by John Gunter that manages to encompass scenes as various as Frankfurt Airport (with myriad lights twinkling in the background) and Greenham Common with awesome missiles*

*behind the barbed-wire compound. Stephen Oliver's score also
combines martial ferocity with plangent melancholia.*
Michael Billington, 'Map of the Left', *The Guardian*, 22 Oct. 1983

Maydays is about being a socialist in Britain today. To understand the
New Right you've got to understand defectors. There are the class kind
like Norman Tebbit and Roger Scruton and then there are the political
kinds like Paul Johnson and Hugh Thomas. I feel, although we failed to
create a working-class audience, we have an audience which we've
brought along with us. They're teachers, social workers, union officials,
and the like. I felt that one should write plays for them. Plays about the
problems rather than plays that are didactic or proselytize. . . . There's
still this syndrome on the left that says you mustn't wash your dirty
linen in public.

Edgar, quoted in Kevin Cully, 'Self Criticism and the Stage',
Tribune, 27 Apr. 1984, p. 13

The paradox of defection is that the one thing people retain is the reason
they left. Most people leave revolutionary parties, and communist
parties in particular, because they joined out of ideals of liberation and
freedom, but find that communism in operation is authoritarian. But
what they take over with them is authoritarianism. . . . The mistake that
the left always make is to leave the question of human nature open to be
defined by the right, because Marxism is supposed to be a science and
human behaviour a function of material circumstance. We presently
have two definitions of human nature, that people are entirely motivated
by personal greed and by atavistic tribalism, spending their days making
money and their nights supporting West Ham or the Task Force. If there
is a message in *Maydays*, it is that the urge to protest, the urge to resist,
and the outrage at injustice are just as human.

Edgar, quoted in Francesca Simon, 'The Urge to Protest',
New Society, 20 Oct. 1983, p. 106-7

I wanted to look at how much the much publicized shift to the right
looks from the insides of the skulls of people in mid-flight (or, in the
case of Alliance supporters, in mid-leapfrog). And, as in *Destiny*, I
wanted to show my defectors as recognizable people with recognizable
concerns, and, perhaps unlike *Destiny*, concerns that would directly
touch the type of audience which attends the Barbican Theatre. But,
again, I didn't want the play merely to be a series of psychological case
studies — I wanted to set three generations of defectors within an

analysis of the 25 years of history covered by the play. So what I hoped would happen was that the audience would recognize the characters from the inside, but be able, simultaneously, like a sudden film-cut from close-up to wide-angle, to look at how these individual journeys were defined by the collective journey of the epoch.

Edgar, 'Public Theatre in a Private Age',
The Second Time as Farce, p. 172

Of course it is essential that socialists face up to their mistakes and the mistakes of the past. Without this the future is doomed. But to do so as Edgar does, to demolish the left with only vague hints now and then that the left has also been responsible for some very positive things, becomes frustrating and infuriating. . . . The longer I watched the play, the more I felt that Edgar's jibes at the left arose from a sense of personal enmity.

Misha Glenny, '*Maydays* Turns on the Left',
Tribune, 28 Oct. 1983

He writes a history of our times around the notion that between 1968 and 1975 a revolution in Britain was necessary, possible, desirable, and betrayed. The politics of the play are thus a politics of fantasy bearing scant relation to what was actually happening in the world and in Britain during that time, and to the aspirations and preoccupations of real people. In the scene in which one figure renounces the revolution, another character declares he has joined the Labour Party. The only passing mention of it in three-and-a-half hours. The news is received with mocking scorn.

Peter Jenkins, 'How to Play around with the Politics of Fantasy',
The Guardian, 26 Oct. 1983, p. 17

Edgar ignores almost completely what is of direct political concern to the majority of his audience — parliamentary democracy. Most of them have always rejected as silly and/or dangerous the antics of the extreme left (if not always their work in the theatre) *and* the authoritarianism of the right of the Tory party, while admiring the courage of East European dissidents. Edgar's humorous, and, at times, guilt-ridden reappraisal of past would-be revolutionaries, though based on intimate inside knowledge, only provides more ammunition to those who mock from without; and thus undermines his avowed intention to give a greater understanding of why people protested, albeit futilely or absurdly, in order to cherish what he still regards as worthwhile radical protest — nuclear disarmament, women's and blacks' rights, etc. *Maydays* will encourage most of its audience not to engage with its political relevance, but to retain a smug distance from it. This distancing is reinforced by Edgar's choice of dramatic form. Though often cleverly engineered and greatly extended by the RSC's resources of actors and machinery, the fringe theatre techniques of rapid juxtapositions of time and place are better at satirically pointing out the ironies of changed positions than giving a profound subjective understanding of individual motivation.

Andrew Hislop, 'Children of the Would-Be Revolution', *Times Literary Supplement*, 28 Oct. 1983

It is — at its best — stimulating, revelling in the breadth of its theme, firing off ideas in profusion. But it is also the work of a mind struggling, at great length, to explain the left's crisis of direction, and does not wholly escape the charge of being navel-contemplation, private soul-searching of limited appeal. The progress through Martin's youth of communes and protests, each scene with a full complement of characters and ideological debates, seems like the left's answer to *Cavalcade* and its most interesting developments are kept back until the third and fourth hours, when they are hardest to digest.

Irving Wardle, *The Times*, 22 Oct. 1983

Edgar has so much plot to get in that he has to resort continually to the long, measured speech which, obligingly, nobody interrupts. Verbal smartness, gags about the barmy sectarianism, the party newspapers, the chronic inability actually to organize anything, all lighten the narrative but leave it somehow literary and earthbound. And in the long central sections there are too few surprises in the perceptions. . . . What is more encouraging is Edgar's vision of socialism as a kind of baton being passed on in a relay race. It doesn't matter if runners fall by the wayside or join another team if somebody else takes over. If his view that the current runners are the feminists is contentious because liberation — freedom — is not a synonym for socialism, well, the point he is trying to make is precisely that it ought to be. But what lifts the whole play into a richer and headier dimension is the 'Russian' strand to the story.

Paul Allen, 'Passing the Baton', *New Statesman*, 28 Oct. 1983

Maydays is not by any means a perfect play, in form, historical accuracy or personal or political insight, but it is a play by which all others on the theme of modern political history may well come to be judged.

Steve Grant, *Plays and Players*, Dec. 1983, p. 18

See also:

Michael Billington, '*Maydays* Manifesto', *The Guardian*, 28 Oct. 1983,
  p. 10.

Bernard Crick, 'David Edgar Catches Peter Jenkins's Ear at the
  Barbican', *Essays on Politics and Literature* (Edinburgh University
  Press, 1989), p. 251-3.

Tony Dunn, 'Writers of the Seventies', *Plays and Players*, June 1984,
  p. 35-6. [*Maydays* and Howard Barker's *Victory*.]

'Paul Foot Savages David Edgar's *Maydays*', *New Socialist*, No. 15
  (Jan.-Feb. 1984), p. 45-6.

Entertaining Strangers

A community play in two acts, commissioned by the Colway Theatre
  Trust.
First production: St. Mary's Church, Dorchester, Dorset, 18 Nov. 1985
  (dir. Ann Jellicoe).
First London production: Cottesloe Th., 9 Oct. 1987 (dir. Peter Hall;
  with Judi Dench as Sarah Eldridge and Tim Pigott-Smith as Henry
  Moule).
Published: Methuen New Theatrescript, 1986; revised, in *Plays: One*.

*His script covers the period 1829 to 1873 and concentrates on
the evolution of two local notables: the founder of the brewers
Eldridge Pope, Sarah Eldridge, and the hell-fire vicar who did
intermittent battle with her, Henry Moule. She is, to be honest,
not the most interesting of characters, spending (as she does)
most of the play cannily expanding her business, transforming
herself from publican to gentlewoman, and interacting with the
other members of her increasingly prosperous clan. But he is
absolutely fascinating, the sort of Victorian you instinctively
find yourself describing in geological terms: flinty integrity;
granite determination; rock-like obduracy. As played in old age
by the conscientiously craggy John Hanson, he even looks as if
he's been carved on Mount Rushmore. There's some swapping
of roles as the evening proceeds; and when we meet Moule he's
Rod Drew, a more modestly sculpted gentleman. But the
personality is already formed. He alienates the poor of his new
parish by refusing to continue paying communants for*

swigging the wine with shouts of 'Cheers, Lord', and he drives away the rich, by inveighing as intransigently against their gambling and blaspheming as against the local whores and drunks. 'Sin is sin', he bluntly opines, 'its wages death'. yet when disaster strikes, he's still there, dogmatically dependable to the last. So far from accepting an invitation to escape the cholera epidemic of 1854, he almost singlehandedly prevents it spreading from the outlying slums into the town of Dorchester: collecting clothes from the dead, boiling them clean, visiting the sick and dying, offering them sympathy without compromise: 'sin is an abomination and his child is cursed for ever more', he characteristically informs the sister of a comatose harlot, not without grief. Edgar is large-minded enough to respect this grim do-gooder, but right-minded enough not to let his respect cloud his judgment. The play's perspective is, as you'd expect, defiantly socialist. Much is heard and seen of spoiled and uncaring nobs, exploited labourers and brutalized women, families crammed into tiny, dank hovels. Indeed, the point of the piece is embodied in its title. Far from 'suspecting people who have more time for the needs of utter strangers than for those they know', as Sarah admits to doing in Act One, perhaps we should entertain strangers, 'rescue them, snatch them from the very jaws of hell', as she comes tentatively to believe in Act Two. She's converted from one stance to the other by Moule's exemplary selflessness. Moule changes too, up to a point. Early on, he sermonizes about the scriptural duty of servants to obey their masters: his experiences during the plague, when fathers must continue earning their pittance in the fields whether or not their children are dying at home, leave him thinking rather more of masters' obligations to their servants. He's a man of his time; his religion is a sort of gunboat Christianity; but at least the barrels end pointing in roughly the right direction. The impression left by the evening, though, is far from dourly didactic. It's always busy and energetic, often festive. . . . The action switches from platform to platform and, at more spectacular moments, from them to the floor below. Exotic pub signs — a criss-cross of mops, spades, sickles, for instance — appear from nowhere. On come the fingerbowl classes in their carriages, or the yokels in their harvest parade, or a line of great, gaudy, vaguely Turkish puppets

*commemorating the allied achievements in the Crimea. Or up
go fairground ads ('test your strength'), a frockcoated gent
blunders past you mumbling 'where's the beer tent?', on lollop
human horses with brightly dressed boys on their shoulders, and
we're at the Dorchester races.*

Benedict Nightingale, *New Statesman*, 29 Nov. 1985, p. 43

Entertaining Strangers was written for a vast but (as I wrote) indeter-
minate number of people, all of whom were rightly to expect not only a
part but a name, an age, and, preferably, an address. Two devices arose
out of these exigencies. The first was that certain parts — mostly but not
exclusively among the larger ones — were split, with one performer
playing the younger and another the older self. This gave rise to various
theatrical possibilities which have made this doubling (or, perhaps more
accurately, halving) an essential part of the dramatic vocabulary of the
play. Second, a significant proportion of the story is told through
narrative — most of it delivered by specific, named individuals (whether
participants in or observers of a particular scene), but some distributed
more generally among members of the company. . . . It is impossible to
over-estimate the importance of the research work undertaken for the
play. In particular, it meant that almost every character actually existed,
and their names, ages, addresses, and relations were not easily invented,
but patiently culled from microfilm, ledger, and in several cases
gravestone.

Edgar, 'Author's Note', *Entertaining Strangers*, p. 7

The megalomaniac appeal of a company of 150-plus soon fades as you
grapple with the problems of finding something real for all of them to
do. . . . There is in [community plays] the possibility of creating a sort
of theatre that once existed in this country but which was gradually
dissipated and fragmented by the pressures of commerce and careerism.
In the late 'sixties and early 'seventies, there was a remarkable alliance
— artistic as well as ideological — between the two great traditions of
twentieth-century radical theatre: between the surreal, the symbolic, and
the absurd on the one hand, and the polemical, the didactic, and the
Brechtian on the other. In Britain this took the form, particularly in the
various festivals which were then such an important aesthetic exchange,
of a clear and generous cross-fertilization between the work of the
basically university-educated political playmakers who founded groups
like 7:84, Portable Theatre, and Joint Stock; and the groups, usually
consisting of art school graduates, who defined themselves as perform-

ance artists. . . . What Ann Jellicoe has created over the years are not plays or pageants, but kinds of carnival, and it is that reality which provides the sense of an event not just of commitment and energy but of moral force and artistic scale.

Edgar, 'All Aboard the A-Train and Join the Carnival',
The Guardian, 16 Nov. 1985, p. 11

It didn't take me too much time — though I suspect it would have taken a more assiduous reader of the works of Mikhail Bakhtin even less — to realize that my play is a kind of theatrical carnival. And in rewriting the play for production at the National Theatre — a project minutely informed by a belated but painstaking reading of *Rabelais and His World* — I have increased and I hope deepened its carnivalesque character. . . .

One of the remarkable things about proto-carnival theatre as I experienced it in St. Mary's Church, Dorchester, is its amazing flexibility. Somehow, because in the promenade form the audience is able to choose what to look at, to construct its own spatial relationship with the event, it is able to switch not just the direction but the very *mode* of its attention, if not in the twinkling of an eye, then certainly in the turn of a head. Perhaps in fact I shouldn't have been so surprised. It's the custom of theatrical snobs like myself to complain of the exponentially diminishing concentration span of the TV remote control generation, but to forget the positive side of that phenomenon, which is an extraordinary quickness of uptake, a learned capacity to click into highly contrasted narratives and indeed moods at a moment's notice. Most of us had had the sense, watching even quite modern realist plays (and certainly in Ibsen), that the audience is way ahead of the exposition, that while the plot's still *en route* the punters have already arrived. In *Entertaining Strangers*, the audience evinced a remarkable capacity to switch its attention and its mode of perception from a race-meeting to a church, from a participatory drinking song to the witness of a silent man at prayer.

Edgar, 'Festivals of the Oppressed',
The Second Time as Farce, p. 236, 241-2

The story we hit upon — of a titanic if historically unlikely twenty-year contest of wills between a fundamentalist pastor and a businesswoman — gave ample opportunity to explore the tension at the heart of the mid-nineteenth century period, a tension I'd already touched on in *Nickleby*, between feudal atavisms and commercial energies, between the ancient mysteries of the countryside and contemporary certainties of town. . . .

In the course of *Entertaining Strangers*, the cleric Henry Moule discovers an almost superhuman care for strangers, but he cannot apply this lesson to relations with his own son. While the brewer Sarah Eldridge, desperately loving of her own, cannot extend that love beyond her doors. It seems to me clear that both forms of love are limited and insufficient. The first has blighted the socialist experiment, the second challenges the moral pretensions of the enterprise culture.

Edgar, 'Introduction', *Plays: Two*, p. xii

It has been wonderful to have had a long rehearsal period at the National to re-examine the play and take it apart. I have found it difficult to de-programme Dorchester and re-programme it without losing the spirit the show had there. The most obvious change has been to slim the cast from 188 to 23. This may sound extreme, but I have reduced the play to 50 characters and there is now considerable doubling up. In some ways, this has been an advantage, because it has allowed me to develop the central characters more fully and to deepen the story-line.

Edgar, quoted in Judy Clifford, 'Character Deeply Dug', *The Times*, 14 Oct. 1987

[In reworking the play for the National Theatre] I realized early on that I would need to create some kind of metaphorical surrogate for the sheer power of Dorchester's numbers (and the emotional strength of the fact that the play was performed in a church established by one of the central characters, within a stone's throw of a brewery founded by the other). In outline, *Entertaining Strangers* is about the attempt to impose two eminently Victorian values on an English country town in the process of transformation from an essentially rural to an urban society. Both sets of beliefs are found wanting in face of the older and more basic realities which emerge to challenge them during the course of the play. These realities — and the ancient mysteries that both acknowledge and confront them — are represented in the new version by fragments from a mummers' play, which is sometimes actually happening, but more often takes the form of a snatch or echo in the mind.

Edgar, 'Introduction', *Plays: Two*, p. 388

Two years ago I saw David Edgar's *Entertaining Strangers* in St. Mary's Church, Dorchester, with a cast of 180. Now the play has been reworked to become a Peter Hall promenade production at the Cottesloe and the contrast is fascinating. What you lose, inevitably, is the moving sense of a community coming to terms with its own past: what you gain is a greater sense of dramatic focus and the high definition skill of the professional actor. In Dorchester I was moved to tears: at the Cottesloe I looked on with admiration. The main point is, however, that a community play has been shown to have a national relevance. . . . Hall's production harks back to his film of *Akenfield* in its recreation of rural ritual. The communal moments are some of the most impressive, with Mr. Dudley's twin bridges advancing upon the audience bearing the fairground sideshows of Dorchester races, or, at one point, a giant Stephenson-like steam-engine symbolizing the opening up of this hitherto-closed world. . . .

Tim Pigott-Smith's Moule is a figure of Brand-like severity and harshness who undergoes a profound spiritual change as he sees Fordington visited by what he takes to be three angels of death with a copper-boiler. But the supreme virtue of his performance is that he enlists sympathy for the character by playing him from his own point of view. And the great merit of Judi Dench's Sarah is that she never seeks to soften or sentimentalize a hard-nosed businesswoman more concerned with striking a deal than tending her injured son. . . . In Dorchester . . . Ann Jellicoe's production struck a note of festal cheer and ended with a utopian hymn to the future. Peter Hall's beautifully-marshalled show is more sombre, bringing out forcefully Victorian rural squalor and the ever-present Hardyesque sense of death and lowering fate.

Michael Billington, 'In the Madding Crowd',
The Guardian, 17 Oct. 1987

The language of debate, the religiosity of period speech — often poor pastiche — and the various blind alleys within the narrative, all combine to produce an admixture that has no consistency. It's as if John Fowles had written a village pantomime for adults. Leftish historical dramatizing rubs shoulders with interludes of sheerest mummerset.

Robert Gore Langton,
Plays and Players, Dec. 1987, p. 23

See also:

Michael Davie, 'By Stage Coach to Dorchester', *The Observer*, 20 Sept. 1987, p. 20. [The London cast of the play visit Dorchester.]

Alan Hurst, '*Entertaining Strangers*', *Thomas Hardy Journal*, IV, No. 2 (May 1988), p. 42-6.

Ann Jellicoe, *Community Plays* (Methuen, 1987).

Tim Pigott-Smith, 'Casting the Community Play', *Drama*, No. 4, 1987 p. 11-12. [National Theatre rehearsals.]

That Summer

A play in two acts.
First production: Hampstead Th., London, 10 July 1987 (dir. Michael
Attenborough).
Published: Methuen, 1987.

*Against the backdrop of the 1984 mineworkers' strike, Howard,
an Oxford don, and his wife Cressida, a chiropractor, have
invited two miners' daughters, Michele and Frankie, to share
their seaside holiday. Also sharing the seaside bungalow are
Terry, a teacher and family friend, and Daniel, Howard's
teenage son by a previous marriage. Over the two weeks they
live together, the relationships produce transformation in the
middle-class adults. Cressida, who had married the vasec-
tomized Howard in part because she did not want children,
learns she has been impregnated during a brief affair with a
'Trot from Cowley' who, like her, is on an Oxford miners'
support committee. Howard ultimately shares her joy: the final
scene, a year after the main action, shows them happily in love,
with child in the background. Terry, for his part, comes out as
homosexual, replacing his pink triangle, a sign of gay pride
which he has never dared wear, with Michele's gift of an NUM
badge. The two working-class teenagers are also transformed:
brought to an appreciation and understanding of new left/liberal
values (Michele has told a 'poof' joke in the first act). This is
further underscored by Alan, Michele's father, who brings the
two girls to the cottage at the beginning of the action and
collects them at the end: in the interim, he has picketed a power
station with no effect on the power workers, but with the aid of
anarchists and gays who, though 'unhygienic' were, in comparison with the power workers throwing pennies at the miners,
'all right'. The play has thus opened the door to two new rooms,
as its own imagery puts it. The first has in it the salvation of
middle-class radicalism, jaded (in the figure of Howard) and
confused (in the figure of Cressida): they are given life by the
strike, their barrenness made fertile. The second contains the
widening of the vision of the working-class characters, who
blithely discriminate against such people as Terry but who, in*

adversity, come to realize who their true friends are. It is the dramatic fusion of the working class at its most militant with the 'new social forces' — ethnic minorities, gay people, women.

John Lloyd, *Times Literary Supplement*, 24 July 1987, p. 796

It seems in retrospect, and paradoxically, that the most important thing to come out of that great collective endeavour [of middle-class support for the miners' strike] was the growth of personal relationships; not only among the activists (and particularly the wives), but also between them and their outside supporters in the cities and elsewhere. And why those relationships were genuinely inspirational was surely because they changed not only people's view of each other (the constant refrain of *surprise*), but also their view of themselves. . . . I felt it too, in my own limited — but happily sustained — contacts with the group of South Wales mining families which inspired my play. And I'm sure that's the reason why — to my *considerable* surprise — I appear to have written a play set against the background of a year-long national struggle, covering the length and breadth of the country and touching the lives of millions, with a cast of only seven, six scenes, and one set. I am convinced, however, that this foray into the strange and, for me, hitherto uncharted territory of naturalistic comedy arises out of the deepest reality of what at least some of those millions actually *experienced*; what that year was really about: the building of personal relationships in action (nay, even 'forged in struggle') in a way that strengthened as well as challenged the participants, whatever the immediate outcome.

Edgar, 'To Have and Have Not,
City Limits, 2 July 1987, p. 12

The two major, strange new features of the miners' strike, both a consequence of its length, were, one, the movement among the wives, and the other, the personal relationships that were struck up between the miners and the people in urban England. . . . The new factor was those relationships — everybody has stories, and all the strike literature comments on it. So how do you deal with it? You put people in a house together, in a confined space, and watch the sparks fly. It's a traditional dramatic way of representing. . . . The form of a social comedy is the correct form for the play.

Edgar, quoted in Mick Martin, 'Selfishness versus Compassion',
Plays International, Oct. 1987, p. 20

That Summer falls prey to the peculiar self-dramatizing love-hate-guilt about being middle class which is characteristic of British playwrights of the left.

Victoria Radin, 'The Pit and Pendulum',
New Statesman, 24 July 1987

Edgar is the theatrical equivalent of a photo journalist. He reports on the state of the country in the robust prose of a concerned correspondent but fatally lacks the impulse to make art of his material. . . . His characters altogether lack passion. They address each other in the tired language of undergraduate political discussion. The overall effect is the equivalent of painting a picture by numbers of the class divisions in Thatcher's Britain. . . . Howard's holiday is made by discovering one of the girl's grandmothers is Spanish, and settled in Swansea having escaped the bombing of Guernica in 1937. It's that sort of schematic, didactic little left-wing play that passes for serious work in our middle-class theatre.

Giles Gordon, *London Daily News*, 13 July 1987

The even-handedness cancels itself out. Howard the over-articulate don represents jaded political realism and 'sixties nostalgia; wife Cressida upholds gullible yet necessary realism; gay friend Terry has risen from the pits to 'real consciousness'. . . . The all-inclusive representation however yields little insight. It turns out the essential theme is — and I gulp as I pen these words — that Yank sitcom standby, 'the learning experience'. Negating the controversial, this curiously non-interventionist mediation gets carried by its peerless comedy-of-Islington-manners construction. Heavily ironic (irony being the aesthetic of the age, mainly to dampen self-knowledge's sting), the script engineers knee-jerk laughs from how convoluted dialectic theorizing is. Frederic Raphael meets *Armchair Theatre*. . . . Is the oft-brilliant David Edgar, a British theatre prestige touchstone, bucking to become the socialist Neil Simon?

John Lyttle, *City Limits*, 16 July 1987

If Edgar has a talent for charting the inauthentic, what he himself lacks is a convincing theatrical language of belief. Eventually, despite the constant undercutting, Edgar's characters stand up and declare. They all have a set-piece to deliver and each one is shot through with the same awkward, mawkish inauthenticity that Edgar is so skilful, elsewhere in the play, at showing up. This failing may form part of a larger critical debate about the nature of bourgeois culture (and theatre) but Edgar shows no sign of 'placing' this problem in this work. These speeches come from the hearts of his characters (there is a would-be touching declaration from the closet gay Terry), but they all sound as if they come straight from the homilectic packet.

Christopher Edwards, 'Culture Clash',
The Spectator, 25 July 1987

'You are convinced they'll eat the food?' a socialist don asks his wife, in David Edgar's acutely enjoyable new play, of the two miners' daughters they've agreed to look after for a summer fortnight during the 1984 strike. It sounds like an enquiry made about some unusual breed of pet. And, initially, Michele and Frankie — working-class teenagers from the Rhondda — are viewed by their middle-class hosts as virtually another species: to be pampered, at a distance. . . . Embarrassment tingles through what at first appears a comedy of incompatibility. High-minded Howard whinges as the girls chorus, to the tune of 'Early in the Morning', what they'd like to do to the working miners ('Sling 'em to the bottom of the nearest pit shaft'). Cressida winces as her guests explain they've done O-Levels not CSEs as she's patronizingly assumed. With alert wit, Edgar demonstrates how dialogue can divide. 'We don't get half of what you say', blurts Michele, revealing — in a scene that typifies the play's balance of the funny and the sobering — that she and Frankie cower in their bedroom trying to think of passable remarks to make to their bemusingly loquacious hosts. Howard, intelligently played by Oliver Cotton, favours a mandarin idiom of serpentine sentences and dry witticisms. Cressida, beautifully caught by Jessica Turner, roughs-up her nicely-spoken conversation — 'I kind of work and everything' — but condescension is still audible in the parody lower-class accent she adopts.

Partly, *That Summer* is an ironic, observant comedy of manners and an unusual kind of Two Nations drama. Tremors are recorded as the kimono-and-cafetière left collides with representatives from the world of real underprivilege: two bright teenage girls whose lives of already restricted opportunity are now savagely being cut back further. 'Last new thing until we've won', Frankie beamingly confides of the new trainers her mother has bought her for this holiday. Both girls laugh openly at the assumption that they'll be able to pursue any career they like. Even within socialist solidarity, we see, there are deep, continuing divides. Ultimately, though, the play is about making connections. As guests and hosts start to learn from and about each other, some social prejudices fall. Howard and Cressida become conscious of their confining smugness. Michele — at first causing consternation over the quiche by her taste for jokes about queers, illustrated by limp-wrist mimings — is steered beyond such stereotypes by a gay chum of

Cressida's. Rapport between the generations increases too. And there's a sub-plot about marital relations being pulled closer under challenge. . . .

Portraying just one fortnight in Wales during the 1984 miners' strike, *That Summer* also adroitly opens up wider perspectives, indicating links between the hopes and fears of that time, and earlier climactic moments in the annals of the left: the General Strike, the Spanish Civil War, 1968. Edgar never lets his drama simplify into ideological diagram, though. . . . This elegant, humane play keeps its emphasis on the modest but fruitful results that can ensue when diverse lives briefly brush against each other.

Peter Kemp, The Independent, 13 July 1987

Vote for Them

A television play in three one-hour parts, written in collaboration with
  Neil Grant.
Television production: BBC-2, 2, 9, 16 June 1989 (dir. James Ormerod).
Published: BBC, 1989, with Introduction by Neil Grant.

An account of the soldiers' Mock Parliament which met in Cairo in 1943-44, promoting progressive ideas among the troops and worrying the authorities — an episode now virtually forgotten.

Because there's two of us, our work process has been an unusually pure example of the making of a documentary drama. Neil is an academic with a particular interest in war radicalism, and he discovered and researched the true history of the Cairo Forces' Parliament, literally handing over his piles of photocopied speeches and agendas — and his miles of audiotape — for me to have my wicked dramatic way with. I, on the other hand, quickly forgot the specific roles of actual people (not easy; they included Leo Abse) in favour of my fictional versions. Initially, the process was a matter of connecting the various factual things we knew (mostly about the five sessions of the actual parliament) to make them humanly and narratively credible, in the manner of the child connecting dots to make a recognizable picture. Increasingly, however, this storytelling-by-numbers gave way to real dramatizing: my fictional characters gaining independent life and development. . . . If our play starts from a historico-journalistic truth, it doesn't end there. Like any other television play, its ultimate credibility is based on its internal dramatic coherence, on whether it rings imaginatively true with the viewer's experience.

> Edgar, 'Faction Plan', *The Listener*, 1 June 1989, p. 14

Episode one, unfortunately, merely gave Edgar the chance to tick a few items off his dogma sheet, and I have been more gripped by party political broadcasts. Maybe this was no more than a philosophical set-up for more spectacular fireworks to come.

> Patrick Stoddart, 'Singer with Soul Full of Glasnost',
> *Sunday Times*, 4 June 1989, 'Screen', p. 1

Everything in it that was serious, judicious, and diligent was undermined by its worthy, dogged, and bald aspects. Edgar's work has always had a slight tendency to dramatic innocence, as if advancing the argument excuses all manner of stunning lack of realism in the story. Here, a representative young AC2 was treated almost as if a holy fool by seasoned old politicos in the desert army. . . . The child even rose to P. M. in the parliament and, from cold, gave a pivotal speech, a development so unconvincing you fell to pondering how it could have got right through the production process to the screen without somebody noticing. . . . The supreme point of the story — it's the kind of story that makes points — could hardly be more pertinent: that nothing is sovereign over procedure, that regulation is the thin red line against dictatorship. James Ormerod directed the trio with care but without much flair and, among a huge and often strange cast, I want to single out James Grout whose bullish brigadier was done with great wit and economy and, you gradually realized, astonishing subtlety and cunning.

> W. Stephen Gilbert, *Plays and Players*, Aug. 1989, p. 42

Vote for Them ended with one of the most exhilarating accounts of decency making a last stand against institutionalized oppression that you could find outside a film of the 'thirties. The Brigadier invaded the soldiers' 'parliament', ready to use his military police if necessary to outlaw this subversive experiment in democracy. The magic of ritual halted him for a time. 'I spy strangers!' cried out the 'Chancellor of the Exchequer', invoking the traditional defence against intruders. The Brigadier was outmanoeuvred by the Speaker who managed to frame the official interdiction within the sitting of Parliament. This put the application of the ban on to any future parliaments, but not to this last brave stand. When the Speaker declared coolly that he would 'rule' on the military order, the Brigadier gave a start of indignant alarm; and it was impossible to restrain deep satisfaction at the Brass being outwitted. There then followed a debate on democratic rights and social hopes (beautifully paced), in which the actors managed to recapture perfectly the mentality of a kind of very innocent, very generous-minded and very hopeful Englishman who appears long gone. . . . Its topical value has probably not yet fully sunk in.

Peter Lennon, 'Democracy's Last Stand',
The Listener, 22 June 1989, p. 38

Heartlanders

A community play in two acts, with a cast of 300, 'to celebrate
    Birmingham's centenary', written in collaboration with Stephen Bill
    and Anne Devlin.
First production: Birmingham Repertory Th., 19 Oct. 1989 (dir.
    Chris Parr).
Published: Nick Hern Books, 1989.

People come together at Digbeth coach station, Birmingham, when they miss their bus: Aan, looking for a girl he once met in India; Joel, from Jamaica; Margaret, middle class, from Oswestry, leaving a husband and looking for a runaway daughter; Tom, half-heartedly seeking a missing wife, who befriends the pregnant young Rose. The characters' adventures in 28 scenes take them all over the city: a park, Wild West Night at a disco, a pre-natal class, the Exhibition Centre. Multi-racialism is celebrated, ending with 'the ritual of the Diwalli is turning into Christmas'.

The *Heartlanders* audience hardly laughed at the clodhopping 'jokes' in the fifth-rate soap. The best of these was a running (crawling?) gag about a musician lost in the city's labyrinth of subways. The production, in which the 'amateur' actors are better than the 'professional' writers, is fatally slowed up by numerous clunking scene changes. . . . This kind of patronizing writing places the characters in emotive situations, but by keeping the tone of the play resolutely jokey and keeping the story trotting briskly on, refuses to allow the characters space to breathe. So the initially hostile Asian family do a nifty U-turn about their daughter marrying a white; the runaway daughter finds her natural mother and leaves her adoptive parents, but their grief is never shown. Or even hinted at.

Vera Lustig, 'Slumming in Brum', *Plays and Players*, Dec. 1989, p. 23

b: Radio Plays for Schools

Four plays, each of twenty minutes: for the *Inquiry* series.

The Owners *(March 1974), set in a motorcycle factory, and concerned with different forms of company ownership.*

Bad Buy *(April 1975), in which the retailer of a faulty record-player is taken to court.*

Hero or Villain? *(March 1975), a comedy about the different attitudes to crime shown by an old lag and his son, a crooked financier.*

Do Something — Somebody *(May 1977), about a community campaign to block off a road that is being heavily used by through-traffic.*

c: Film Script

Lady Jane

Released: 1986 (dir. Trevor Nunn; with Helena Bonham Carter as Lady Jane Grey, Sarah Kestelman as Frances Grey, Jane Lapotaire as Queen Mary, and John Wood as the Duke of Northumberland). *Unpublished.*

Lady Jane Grey, who at fifteen was used as a pawn in a coup

*masterminded by the 'protestant' party, led by the Duke of
Northumberland, is played by Helena Bonham Carter. . . .
Under pressure from the anti-Papists, the dying teenage King
Edward VI morally blackmails Lady Jane into marrying
Guilford, Northumberland's drunken yobbo son. As played by
Bonham Carter, Lady Jane is a protestant priss: scholarly,
spiky, and (this is the actress's trade mark) sulky. She has to be
literally beaten by her mother into marrying Cary Elwes —
Guilford — who resembles a low-grade Sloanie with a taste for
whores and bad liquor. But — according to David Edgar's
script — these two black sheep find a simple, pure love which
almost transforms the face of England by their radiance and, of
all things, radicalism. Amid the pushing and shoving of the
plotters, Lady Jane is crowned and she and her husband determine that their love shall be shared by the suffering populace.
There are one or two quite embarrassing, because unprepared
for, scenes where Bonham Carter and Elwes euphorically lay
their plans for abolishing inflation, branding for beggary, and
several other social illnesses.*

Clancy Sigal, *The Listener*, 5 June 1986, p. 35-6

If *A Man for all Seasons* is the thinking nun's *Sound of Music*, *Lady
Jane* is the romantic leftist's *Private Life of Henry VIII*.

Philip French, *The Observer*, 1 June 1986

See also:
Elisabeth Dunn, 'Trevor's Head on the Block?', *Sunday Times*, 9 Dec.
1984, p. 54. [On the filming.]

3: Non-Dramatic Writing

Short Stories

'1997', *Marxism Today*, Jan. 1984; reprinted in *The Second Time as
Farce* (1988), p. 248-65.
'Novel Approaches', *Marxism Today*, Aug. 1989, p. 19-23, 25, 27.

[For articles and essays, see Section 5, below.]

The new theatre must be almost everything the old theatre is not. It must be serious in content, but accessible in form. It must be popular without being populist. It must be orientated towards a working-class audience. It must be temporary, immediate, specific, functional. It must get out of theatre buildings. It must be ideological, and proud of it. It must be celebratory (try to convince the Catholic Church that there's no function in 'preaching to the converted'!) It must not be escapist; it must take our times by the throat.

'David Edgar Comments', *Contemporary Dramatists*, ed. James Vinson (St. James Press, 1977), p. 236

What I'm trying to do is paint public life — people at work, living in a social world — with the kind of complexity and ambiguity that theatre has traditionally employed in looking at the domestic world. . . . Everyone now accepts that plays won't send people out to the barricades. What they can do is ultimately give people new images with which to understand the world. But only in connection with their own experience. And that's quite nice, because I'm not a central political committee.

Interviewed by Victoria Radin, 'Fair-Play Playwright', *The Observer*, 8 May 1977, p. 30

What we need to do is to create a style for the presentation of public life. Going right back to why do people go to the theatre: because they are curious, because they want to see other people, because they want to extend their experience into those areas where they cannot extend it by direct experience. Which meant a number of things: people might enjoy plays about China because they would tell them something they didn't know. Of if we want to know what it was like living in the fifteenth century we can't experience that either, so we go to plays to tell us what it was like. In the same way, we want to see things that are very directly related to us, but which it is very difficult to experience anyone else experiencing. I mean one cannot get inside anyone else's love affair, and we only lose our virginity once, so it's quite important to see other people doing it. In the same way with families, we are fascinated by the way other people behave in families — again it is something we can't observe directly. That seems to be the reason for the stranglehold of domestic subjects; people want to know about it because it extends their experience, or it provides useful information with which they can better their lives. Now it seems to me that public life has become increasingly difficult and complex, obscure and influential. Great public events now influence our lives much more directly and demonstrably. And one of the most important things going on in this country in the last ten years has been wage negotiations. I wanted to create a theatre that could tell about this key, vital factor in our national life. What I wanted to do was create a theatre of public life. . . .

You have two alternatives. You can make things ridiculously simple and partisan — in the sense of getting people to support socialism in the same way as they support Leeds United, on a straight tribal basis, which seems to me not in itself a bad thing, but futile and dangerous because it won't actually lead to the building of socialism. Or you have to struggle to find a way of presenting extremely complex, difficult, precise ideas. I mean we all know that the Bolshevik Revolution happened because in 1903 there had been an obscure debate in an upstairs room in a Highgate pub about the membership rules of the Bolshevik Party. And that is why the Russian Revolution happened. On a very precise level. The ideas are both difficult and precise. If you make them simple and vague you are not in fact expressing the ideas. So the struggle is to find ways of expressing complicated ideas in an accessible form. . . .

I became a social realist. I think the only radical alternative to social realism, which is agitprop, was no longer suitable.

> Interviewed by Catherine Itzin, in *Stages in the Revolution*
> (Eyre Methuen, 1980), p. 144-6

I've only recently had sufficient confidence in the validity of myself as a writer, and the validity of what I have to say about the world in which I live — the world in which *I* live, not the world in which railway workers live, the people about whom I've been writing plays — to try and develop my own voice, to that extent. Basing work on literary conceits as in *Death Story*, or on parodies, like *Dick Deterred*, or on factual material as in the documentaries, was to a certain extent borne out of a consciousness of wanting to find something apart from myself to draw on.

> 'Towards a Theatre of Dynamic Ambiguities',
> *Theatre Quarterly*, No. 33 (Spring 1979), p. 11

The most potent, rich, and in many ways politically acute theatrical statements of the past ten years have been made in custom-built buildings patronized almost exclusively by the middle class. . . . I have seen nothing in touring theatre to compare, in terms of memorable (and therefore *usable*) dramatic power, with the tearing down of the wall at the end of Edward Bond's *Lear*; the decision of the hideous Bagley dynasty to move into the Chinese heroin market in the last act of Howard Brenton and David Hare's *Brassneck*; and the sustained fury of Barry Keeffe's *Gotcha*, in which a working-class teenager holds three teachers hostage in a school box-room by threatening to drop a lighted cigarette into a motorcycle petrol tank.

'Ten Years of Political Theatre, 1968-1978',
Theatre Quarterly, No. 32. (1979), p. 25-33,
reprinted in *The Second Time as Farce*, p. 41

We — who came into the theatre on or about the date of the abolition of theatre censorship and the beginnings of the great expansion of subsidy of the late 1960s and early 1970s — are playwrights of a particular kind. Unlike, say, Arnold Wesker or Brendan Behan, we've tended to choose subject matter that is at some distance from our own experience; unlike Brecht or John Arden or Edward Bond, we've largely written about our own country in the present day or recent past; and unlike Shaw, we have been dealing with a world which, in our view, is, sadly, not teetering on the edge of a rational order. . . .

For those socialist playwrights who not only wanted, but needed, to contribute to the discourse of the left as a whole — to hold a mirror to our side as well as the other — there was in these mean times a further painful conundrum. Do we attempt through our work seriously to participate in the debate that is going on on the left after the major reverses it's suffered — a contribution which would inevitably involve a fair amount of dirty political washing, left twisting slowly in the wind? Or do we view our function as socialist artists as being the palm court orchestra on the *Titanic* — providing at least a little cheer and comfort, a bit of confirmation and even celebration of the old ideals — as our comrades call for lifeboats and the waters lap about our heels? . . .

Buffeted and battered though the old hulk may be, there is life in social realism yet. Indeed, perhaps it is the only current form of political theatre that appears to be able to survive a period in which political ideas in the theatre are so deeply resented. . . . What seems to me most important is the way that, hand in hand with alternative cabaret, performance art has influenced the new feminist theatre (and indeed vice versa) to create a style of presentation of radical ideas which owes little to the increasingly arid forms of cartoon agitprop, but is by contrast wacky and individual and lively and provides at least the basis, perhaps, at last, for a synthesis between the literary, cerebral, intellectually rigorous but visually dry work of the university-educated political playwrights of the 1960s and 1970s, and the visually stunning but intellectually thin experiments of the performance artists in and from the art schools.

'Public Theatre in a Private Age' (1982),
reprinted in *The Second Time as Farce*, p. 161, 166, 172-3, 175

The best review I've ever had was when Michael Billington said that, like Balzac, David Edgar seems to be a secretary for our times. And that defined, rather more precisely than I'd ever defined before, what I'd like to be. I'd like to be a secretary for the times through which I'm living.

Interviewed by Elizabeth Swain, in
David Edgar, Playwright and Politician (New York, 1986), p. 335

a: Primary Sources

Bibliographic particulars of plays published only in individual editions will be found under their respective titles in Section 2.

Collections of Plays

Plays: One. Methuen, 1987. [Contains *Destiny*, *Mary Barnes*, *The Jail Diary of Albie Sachs*, *Saigon Rose*, and *O Fair Jerusalem*.]

Plays: Two. Methuen, 1990. [Contains *Ecclesiastes*, *Nicholas Nickleby*, and *Entertaining Strangers*.]

Shorts. Nick Hern Books, 1989. [Contains *Blood Sports*, *The National Theatre*, *The Midas Connection*, and *Baby Love*.]

Collections of Essays

The Second Time as Farce: Reflections on the Drama of Mean Times. Lawrence and Wishart, 1988. [Reprints 16 pieces written between 1977 and 1988, with a new introduction.]

Articles and Reviews

Edgar has been a prolific journalist, writing more often on politics, the right, and racism than on theatre. A small selection of his articles and reviews follows.

'Against the General Will', *Plays and Players*, May 1973, p. 14-15. [State of fringe theatre.]

'Subsidy', *Gambit*, No. 24 (1974), p. 15-40. [Participant in discussion.]

'Residence Permits', *Plays and Players*, July 1975, p. 16-17. [On being a 'writer-in-residence'.]

'Return to Base', *New Edinburgh Review*, No. 30 (Aug. 1975), p. 2-3. [Political theatre.]

'Socialist Theatre and the Bourgeois Author', *Workers and Writers*, ed. Wilfred van der Will (Department of German, Birmingham University, 1975), p. 81-97.

'New Gothics, Realists, and Phantasists', *Gambit*, No. 29 (1976), p. 5-29. [Participant in discussion: however, Edgar's remarks are attributed to David Hare throughout!]

'Playwriting for the Seventies', *Theatre Quarterly*, No. 24 (Winter 1976-77), p. 35-74. [Participant in discussion].

Review of *The Front* [film], *Socialist Voice*, Mar. 1977.

'Achtung!', *New Review*, Nos. 39-40 (June-July 1977), p. 69-71. [Review of *The National Front*, by Martin Walker.]

'The National Front *Is* a Nazi Front', *Socialist Challenge*, 21 July 1977.

'*Fascism as a Mass Movement*, [by] Mihaly Vajda', *Race and Class*, Autumn 1977, p. 212-13.

Contemporary Dramatists, ed. James Vinson, revised ed. (London: St. James Press, 1977), p. 236-7.

'Recrystallization of the Novel', *The Times*, 26 Nov. 1980, p. 9. [On *Nicholas Nickleby*.]

'*A Worker in a Workers' State,* [by] Haraszti', *Socialist Challenge*, 4 Apr. 1978. [Book review.]

'*The British Right*, ed. N. Nugent and R. King', *Race and Class*, Summer 1978, p. 103-05. [Book review.]

'Why the Front Is beyond the Pale', *Sunday Times*, 1 Oct. 1978.

'U.S. Elections: in the Republican Camp', *Searchlight*, No. 63 (Sept. 1980), p. 3-5; No. 64 (Oct. 1980), p. 3-6; No. 65 (Nov. 1980), p. 9-10.

'Address at Giessen Stadttheater, 30 September 1980', *Anglistentag Giessen 1980*, ed. Herbert Grabes (Grossen-Linden: Hoffmann, 1981), p 179-88.

'Respect for the Writer', *Theatre International*, No. 1 (1981), p. 5-6.

'Against the Mainstream', *Times Literary Supplement*, 11 Sept. 1981, p. 1046. [Review of *At the Royal Court*, ed. Richard Findlater.]

'Putting Politics on Stage', *New Socialist*, No. 2 (Nov.-Dec. 1981), p. 38-41.

'The Lurking Threat to Radical Theatre', *The Guardian*, 20 Mar. 1982, p. 10. [The trial of *The Romans in Britain*, by Howard Brenton.]

'Classic Account', *New Statesman*, 16 Apr. 1982, p. 20. [Review of *The National Front in English Politics*, by Stan Taylor.]

'The Good, Bard, and Ugly', *The Guardian*, 21 May 1982. [Review of *The Royal Shakespeare Company*, by Sally Beauman.]

'What Does Marx Mean to You?', *Marxism Today*, Mar. 1983, p. 31-33.

'Bitter Harvest', *New Socialist*, Sept.-Oct. 1983, p. 19-24. [On the 'New Right'.]

'A Shortsighted View of the Defectors' Decade', *The Guardian*, 29 Oct. 1983, p. 12. [Letter about *Maydays*.]

'Diary', *New Statesman*, 5 Apr. 1985, p. 16 [in Warsaw]; 27 Sept. 1985, p. 19; 6 Dec. 1985, p. 16; 17 Jan. 1986, p. 19; 28 Feb. 1986, p. 17; 4 Apr. 1986, p. 16; 16 May 1986, p. 18; 27 June 1986, p. 16; 15 Aug. 1986, p. 21; 3 Oct. 1986, p. 6.

'Why Pay's the Thing', *The Guardian*, 28 June 1985, p. 13. [The writers' case for spending more on theatre.]

'Shadow in the Sun', *New Statesman*, 9 Aug. 1985, p. 26. [Review of *Year of the King*, by Antony Sher.]

'Re-entering Earth's Atmosphere', *New Statesman*, 13 Sept. 1985, p. 27-8. [Review of *For a Pluralist Socialism*, by Michael Rustin.]

'The Revenger's Tragedy', *New Statesman*, 21 Feb. 1986, p. 22-4. [The Westland affair as drama.]

'Divided They Fall', *New Statesman*, 4 July 1986, p. 29-30. [Review of *Prisoners of the American Dream*, by Mike Davis.]

'Twysided', *New Statesman*, 22 Aug. 1986. [Review of *William Barnes: a Life of the Dorset Poet*, by Alan Chedzoy.]

'The New Nostalgia', *Marxism Today*, Mar. 1987, p. 30-1, 33, 35. [On postmodernism.]

'To Have and Have Not', *City Limits*, 2-9 July 1987. [On *That Summer*.]

'Jingles, Jangles', *Marxism Today*, Jan. 1988, p. 44-5. [On the growing number of musicals in British theatre.]

'Why Clause 28 Should Kindly Leave the Stage', *The Guardian*, 28 Jan. 1988, p. 14. [Letter.]

'When the Hardline is Right', *Marxism Today*, Feb. 1988, p. 30-1.

'It's All Done with Cameras', *New Statesman*, 5 Feb. 1988, p. 28-9. [Review of *Reagan's USA*.]

'The Black Arts', *New Statesman and Society*, 29 July 1988, p. 42-3. [Review of *Storms of the Heart*, ed. Kwesi Owusu, and *Behind the Masquerade*, by Kwesi Owusu and Jacob Ross.]

'Mummers', *Pulp*, Summer 1989, p. 16.

Contemporary Dramatists, fourth edition, ed. D. L. Kirkpatrick (London: St. James Press, 1988), p. 141-2.

'Faction Play', *The Listener*, 1 June 1989, p. 13-14. [On docudrama.]

Interviews

Alison Dunn, 'The Drawing Board Stage', *The Guardian*, 17 July 1973, p. 20. [Edgar's teaching at Leeds Polytechnic and Bingley College of Education.]

Catherine Itzin, 'Theatre, Politics, and the Working Class', *Tribune*, 22 Apr. 1977.

Victoria Radin, 'Fair-Play Playwright', *The Observer*, 8 May 1977, p. 30.

'Exit Fascism, Stage Right', *The Leveller*, No. 6 (June 1977), p. 22-3.

Janet Watts, 'Right Side Up', *The Guardian*, 11 May 1977, p. 10. [On *Destiny*.]

'Towards a Theatre of Dynamic Ambiguities', *Theatre Quarterly*, No. 33 (Spring 1979), p. 3-24; reprinted in *New Theatre Voices of the Seventies*, ed. Simon Trussler (Methuen, 1981), p. 157-71.

Misha Berson, 'The Politics of a Playwright', *Threepenny Review* (Berkeley, Calif.), No. 7 (Fall 1981), p. 25-6.

Sally Beauman, 'David Edgar: Back to the Barricades', *Sunday Times Magazine*, 16 Oct 1983, p. 73, 75, 77, 79.

John Cunningham, 'Signals of Distress', *The Guardian*, 17 Oct. 1983, p. 11.

Francesca Simon, 'The Urge to Protest', *New Society*, 20 Oct. 1983, p. 106-7.

Kevin Cully, 'Self-Criticism and the Stage', *Tribune*, 27 Apr. 1984, p. 13.

Elizabeth Swain, *David Edgar, Playwright and Politician* (New York: Peter Lang, 1986), p. 325-36. [Interview conducted in Sept. 1981, mainly about *Nicholas Nickleby*.]

Mark Lawson, 'Hard Times for the Left', *The Independent*, 8 July 1987, p. 13.

Mick Martin, 'Selfishness versus Compassion', *Plays International*, Oct. 1987, p. 18-20.

Judy Clifford, 'Character Deeply Dug', *The Times*, 14 Oct. 1987, p. 20.

Mark Lawson, 'Left Alone', *The Independent Magazine*, 26 Nov. 1988, p. 46-8.

b: Secondary Sources

Full-Length Study

Elizabeth Swain, *David Edgar, Playwright and Politician* (New York: Peter Lang, 1986).

Articles and Sections in Books

Ronald Hayman, *British Theatre since 1955* (Oxford University Press, 1979), p. 106-13.

Steve Grant, 'Voicing the Protest', *Dreams and Deconstructions: Alternative Theatre in Britain*, ed. Sandy Craig (Ambergate: Amber Lane, 1980), p. 134-8.

Catherine Itzin, *Stages in the Revolution: Political Theatre in Britain since 1968* (London: Eyre Methuen, 1980), p. 139-51.

C. W. E. Bigsby, 'The Politics of Anxiety: Contemporary Socialist Theatre in Britain', *Modern Drama*, XXIV (Dec. 1981), p. 393-403.

Stanley Weintraub, 'David Edgar', *British Dramatists since World War II: Dictionary of Literary Biography, Vol. 13* (Detroit: Gale, 1982), p. 160-70.

John Bull, *New British Political Dramatists* (London: Macmillan, 1984), p. 151-94.

Malcolm Hay, 'David Edgar, Public Playwright', *Drama*, No. 151 (1984), p. 13-16.

Tony Dunn, 'The Play of Politics', *Drama*, No. 2, 1985, p. 13-15.

David Ian Rabey, *British and Irish Political Drama in the Twentieth Century* (London: Macmillan, 1986), p. 175-87.

Richard Allen Cave, *New British Drama in Performance on the London Stage, 1970-1985* (Gerrards Cross: Colin Smythe, 1987), p. 178-9.

Colin Chambers and Mike Prior, *Playwrights' Progress* (Oxford: Amber Lane, 1987), p. 90-5.

Michelene Wandor, *Look Back in Gender* (London: Methuen, 1980), p. 126-34.

Ruby Cohn, 'Shakespeare Left', *Theatre Journal*, XL (Mar. 1988), p. 48-60. [On *Death Story* and *Dick Deterred*.]

Susan Rusinko, *British Drama 1950 to the Present* (Boston: Hall, 1989), p. 136-7.